Key Issues
in e-Learning:
Research and Practice

Also available from Continuum

Key Ideas in Educational Research, Marlene Morrison and
David Scott

Handbook of Online Education, Debra Marsh, Clare Killen and
Shirley Bennett

The e-Assessment Handbook, Geoffrey Crisp

The e-Learning Reader, Jill Jameson and Sara de Freitas

Key Issues in e-Learning: Research and Practice

Norbert Pachler
and Caroline Daly

continuum

Continuum International Publishing Group
The Tower Building   80 Maiden Lane
11 York Road   Suite 704
London   New York
SE1 7NX   NY 10038

www.continuumbooks.com

British Library Cataloguing-in-Publication Data
A catalogue record for this book is available from the British Library.

ISBN: 978-1-8470-6360-1 (paperback)
        978-1-8470-6358-8 (hardcover)

Library of Congress Cataloging-in-Publication Data
Pachler, Norbert.
  Key issues in e-learning : research and practice / Norbert Pachler and Caroline Daly.
      p. cm.
  Includes bibliographical references and index.
  ISBN 978-1-84706-358-8 (hardcover) -- ISBN 978-1-84706-360-1 (pbk.) 1. Internet in education. 2. Information technology. 3. Virtual computer systems. 4. World Wide Web. I. Daly, Caroline. II. Title.

  LB1044.87.P335 2011
  371.33'44678--dc22

                              2010029086

Typeset by Free Range Book Design & Production
Printed and bound in India

Contents

Figures and Tables   vii
Introduction   1

1 The "e" in e-Learning   11
What do we mean by "e-learning"?   11
What is learning?   17
Towards a theory of/for e-learning   18
Policy as a driver for e-learning   19
Potentials and benefits of technology in education   21
What do we mean by e-learning? Revisited   25
Some theoretical considerations   25
The importance of self-regulation and meta-learning   28
e-Learning 2.0?   32
Some additional theoretical considerations   33
Conclusion   35

2 Changing Contexts   37
Introduction   37
Ecology of learning with technologies   38
Technological developments and changing views of
    knowledge and learners   40
Socio-cultural practices   43
Policy-making   45
Policy tensions affecting educational institutions   49
Changing personal/public boundaries   51
Challenges for schools, post-16 colleges and
    universities   54
Conclusion   55

3 Theories, Concepts and Models   57
Introduction   57
The shared construction of knowledge   61

Laurillard's Conversational Framework | 63
Computer-mediated communication | 64
CMC as a literate learning practice | 65
Participation | 67
The individual and agentive dimensions of e-learning | 71
Theoretical perspectives on practitioner development | 75
Conclusion | 78

4   **Online Learning and Teaching and Learning about Online Teaching** | **81**
Learning revisited | 81
Affordance | 83
Knowledge construction through interaction | 83
Supporting collaboration and artefact creation | 85
Distributed cognition? | 87
A sense of place | 90
Pedagogical templates, models and frameworks | 91
Conclusion | 108

5   **e-Assessment, e-Portfolios, Quality Assurance and the Student Experience** | **109**
Introduction | 109
Quality assurance and the student experience | 109
e-Assessment | 111
Some examples of e-assessment practices | 119
e-Portfolios | 122
Conclusion | 126

6   **Researching e-Learning** | **129**
Introduction | 129
Maturation of e-learning research | 130
Researching the learning in e-learning | 135
The "narrative turn" | 138
The Qualitative Content Analysis model | 141
Where next? | 143
The theory–practice challenge for e-learning research | 145

References | 149
Index | 169

Figures and Tables

Figures

0.1 (Unhelpful) Discourses (created with Inspiration 8)   2
0.2 Advances in Communication and Information Resources
for Human Interaction (source: adapted from Borgman et al.,
2008: 11)   3
0.3 The "Whole Picture of E-learning" model (source:
George Siemens, http://www.elearnspace.org/
Articles/wholepicture.htm)   7
1.1 e-learning = enhanced learning (source: JISC, 2004: 10)   15
1.2 e-learning = enhanced learning (source: JISC, 2007: 10)   16
1.3 The conversational framework for the learning process
(source: Laurillard et al., 2000)   26
1.4 The conversational framework for supporting the formal
learning process (source: Laurillard 2007: 160)   27
1.5 Key components of a socio-cultural ecological approach
(source: http://www.londonmobilelearning.net)   28
1.6 Themes of transition in e-learning experiences
(source: http://www.wlecentre.ac.uk/cms/files/projects/
reports/PR_Daly-Pachler-Pickering-Bezemer_2006.pdf)   30
3.1 Pedagogical technological content knowledge. The three
circles, Content, Pedagogy and Technology, overlap to
lead to four more kinds of interrelated knowledge
(source: http://tpack.org/tpck/images/tpck/a/a1/
Tpack-contents.jpg)   77
4.1 Learner-centred psychological principles (source: McCombs
and Vakili, 2005: 1585–6)   101–2
4.2 A model of e-learning (source: Anderson, 2008: 61)   103
4.3 Community of inquiry model (source: http://communities
ofinquiry.com/files/coi_model.pdf)   104
4.4 Conole and Fill's model of learning (source: Conole and
Fill, 2005: 8)   105

4.5 A circle of knowledge building and sharing (source: Brown and Adler, 2008: 28)   107

5.1 Good assessment and feedback practices (source: Nicol, 2007: 3)   112–13

5.2 Word cloud created using Wordle (http://www.wordle.net)   117

5.3 A model of e-portfolio based learning (source: JISC, 2008a: 9)   124

6.1 Co-evolutionary contextual model (source: Andrews and Haythornthwaite, 2007: 40)   135

Tables

0.1 Examples of perceived e-learning technology amplification and reductions (source: Kanuka and Rourke, 2008: 9)   8

1.1 Seven areas of e-learning activity   20

4.1 E-learning pedagogical templates (source: Jara and Mohamad, 2007: 7)   96

4.2 "Parallel" template   97

4.3 Community of inquiry categories (source: Vaughan and Garrison, 2007: 142)   106

5.1 Key aspects of formative assessment (source: Black and Wiliam, 2009: 8)   118

Introduction

"Questions of cost and usefulness dog e-learning": thus read a headline on 4 June 2009 in the *Times Higher Education*.[1] According to the article, which reports on a survey carried out amongst 125 university staff, many academics see e-learning as expensive and time consuming: "it takes much longer to create high-quality e-learning material than to prepare for a traditional form of teaching to achieve the same level of learning and outcome" (p. 9). Another respondent felt that "E-learning is not as good as face-to-face interaction, but it is sometimes a necessity".

At the 2009 conference of the Centre for Excellence in Work-Based Learning for Education Professionals[2] at the Institute of Education, London (9 July) a roundtable discussion about the use of (digital) technology was held in which participants were invited to discuss what they perceived to be "(unhelpful) discourses" in the field. Figure 0.1 sets out which issues came up in the discussion. As can be seen, there are deemed to exist a number of unhelpful discourses dominating the implementation of (digital) technologies, in particular transmission models around the delivery of content or the use of technology for control and management purposes around increased effectiveness. Judging by the comments made by expert discussants on the day, there appear to exist problems in embedding (digital) technologies in existing practices, an issue this book seeks to address. "Perpetual obsolescence" leads to problems around sustainability and often efforts around the introduction of e-learning are framed by a productivity and modernization paradigm. All in all, even if not a comprehensive list, this is a challenging agenda for university staff wanting to implement e-learning.

In this book we explore questions around e-learning with a view to establishing what best be understood by it, mostly with reference to teaching and learning in the context of higher education provision. We also explore why the phenomenon achieved the prominence it has in the last 10 years or so with many providers offering a range of types

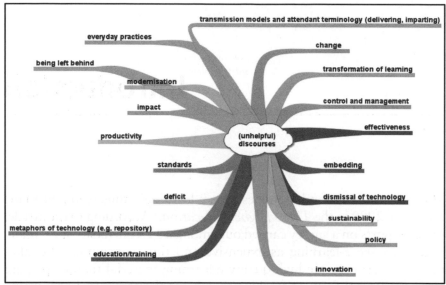

Figure 0.1   (Unhelpful) discourses (created with Inspiration 8)

of provision which make at least some use of (computer-based) digital technologies. And we attempt to delineate e-learning as a discipline by providing a summary and overview of some of the key issues and studies dealing with the phenomenon with reference to relevant research.

We do so because we find that very often the term e-learning is used without ever clearly specifying what is meant by it. In this way people think they are talking about the same thing when this is not necessarily the case, which in turn makes it difficult to achieve synergies and joint understandings that can help practitioners, policy-makers, researchers and managers gain a realistic assessment of the affordances of the investment in time, money and creative thought necessary to exploit the potential of digital technologies to the full. In a sense, therefore, the views of university staff quoted above are not surprising and relate to some fundamental problems of how e-learning is perceived by different stakeholders. Too often digital technologies are "sold" on a false premise of inflated benefits, mostly around efficacy and effectiveness, without due consideration of the disruption they invariably cause to established pedagogical and administrative practices and "technological" and procedural systems and infrastructures. Laurillard (2008a: 524), for example, notes that technology creates an important pressure for change in that it is changing both what we need to know and how we come to know it. Whilst e-learning is invariably not a panacea, it seems essential to engage with these changes. Indeed, society around us is characterized by significant cultural, economic and technological changes and technology is fast becoming an integral part not only of our everyday lives but also, of course, of the higher education landscape (cf. the discussion of the "mobile complex" in Pachler, Bachmair and Cook, 2010). As such, technology has the potential to support higher education in a number of fundamental ways: it can help advance pedagogical practices, processes of teaching and learning, government policy initiatives such as widening participation, financial exigencies of universities such as in the context of the recruitment of international students, resource stringencies such as in the context of the repurposing of material and so on.

The Task Force Report on "Cyberlearning" by the National Science Foundation of America (Borgman et al., 2008; see Figure 0.2 below by Roy Pea and Jillian Wallis) provides a useful overview of the historical advances in ICT for human interaction. It, for us, visualizes at a glance the growing significance of technology in a fundamental human activity, which we consider to be key to (effective) learning and teaching, namely communication. Pea and Wallis discern five waves of resources, which increase in complexity of mediation from basic, physical interaction around transient oral communication towards social networking and

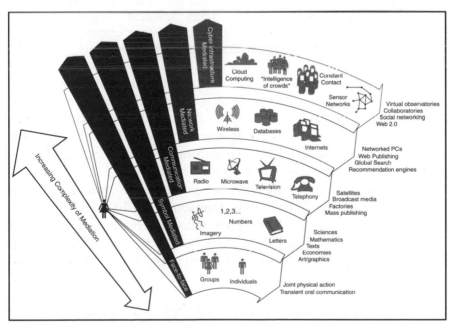

Figure 0.2 Advances in communication and information resources for human interaction
Source: Adapted from Borgman et al., 2008: 11

Web 2.0 characterized by cybernetic mediation, cloud computing, sensor networks etc. With each new wave of mediating technologies the set of actions and interactions possible has changed. University education can simply not afford to stand aside and ignore these developments.

Laurillard (2008a: 527–8) examines applications for 2007 ESRC–EPSRC funding for technology-enhanced learning, which shows a wide variety of possibilities underlining the problems of considering e-learning as a unitary concept:

> Inquiry-based; Construction; Conceptual understanding; Taking tests; Problem-solving; Narrative; Literacy; Game authoring; Techno-computing skill-learning; Fieldwork; Communication; Collaboration; Learning identities; Conceptual networks; Manipulation skills; Informal interests; Self-worth; Modelling; Scenarios; Evaluating evidence.

She goes on to note that the research proposals also identify a wide range of applications, which underlines the complexity of the field:

> Games; Tools; Cultural tools; Adaptive intelligent tutoring systems; Avatars; Embodied interaction; Augmented cognition; Personal learning environments; Learner models; Portable devices; Conversation agents; Editable digital artefacts; Digital data tracking; Haptic devices; Virtual objects; Online communities; Adaptive support; Simulation; Collaborative technology.

Clearly, no single book will be able to do justice to all of these strands. Our main aim, therefore, in this book is to underline the complexity of the field and, at the same time, to focus in on what seems to us to be key principles which underpin and are integral to many of the above aspects of technology-enhanced learning / e-learning. For a discussion of terms and their relationship and definition see Chapter 1.

Another useful contextual reference point is the annual US-based *Horizon Report*. The 2010 edition (Johnson et al., 2010) enumerates a number of key trends which, it argues, reflect the realities at the time of writing this book, the first half of 2010, both in the sphere of academia and in the world at large. They can be seen as drivers for e-learning and are (pp. 3–4):

> • The abundance of resources and relationships made easily accessible via the Internet is increasingly challenging us to revisit our roles as educators in sense-making, coaching and credentialing. ...

- People expect to be able to work, learn and study whenever and wherever they want to.
- The technologies we use are increasingly cloud-based, and our notions of IT support are decentralized.
- The work of students is increasingly seen as collaborative by nature, and there is more cross-campus collaboration between departments.

The UK has seen the publication of the government's *Digital Britain* report in 2009 which, amongst many other things espouses the UK's transformation into "a world leader in research, innovation, technology and creativity, by inspiring the next generation and creating the environment for digital talent to thrive" (BIS and DCMS, 2009: 165). Clearly, universities have a mayor contribution to make if this ambition is to become reality. And e-learning in a university context—as elsewhere—can be seen to be one important dimension of an implementation plan of the report.

It will have become clear by now that the main focus of this book is on e-learning in university contexts with a clear focus on learning and teaching. We are, of course, keenly aware that e-learning also forms an important part of life-long and work-based learning outside the university context. E-learning clearly is a widely used method of training (delivery) in companies and other organizations and not just in the field of IT skills but around many compliance matters, business skills and beyond. Often issues around technological "solutions" and content have been in the foreground in these contexts and only as the focus of the online training changes to more complex areas does the focus on processes and pedagogy come into focus. Rapid advances in technology, for example around wireless technologies and portable devices increase the flexibility of the media used. While a number of these trends clearly resonate with the university sector, such as the increased flexibility afforded by technology including the growing prominence of social media tools, we focus in this book on curriculum-orientated, pedagogically mediated interventions.

These opening statements have hopefully addressed any questions that may have existed around "Why e-learning?" If not, Chapters 1 and 2, exploring what e-learning is as well as the context in which it takes place, will hopefully do so. Yet, readers may ask themselves "Why *another* book about e-learning? Have the last few years not seen a proliferation of publications in this field?" Yes, we have certainly seen a proliferation of titles on e-learning of late. Upon closer examination, though, it seems that there are very few authored books that attempt a holistic approach such as we do; most are edited volumes that bring together examples from research and practice without really weaving them into a greater whole. If they do, as, for example, Garrison and Anderson in their very interesting and valuable book (2003), they tend to focus on one particular perspective on the field, in this case the notion of a community of inquiry. Many of the titles about e-learning are of the "how to" variety. Again, such books have a legitimate place in the market but, as Goodyear diagnoses, many of them "so simplify the world that one wonders about their possible relations with action" (2009: vii). This is a view shared by Beaudoin (2008: 123) for the cognate field of distance education:

> To this book review editor, it seems that there is an overabundance of "how to" handbooks being published. Although these are certainly useful to the growing number of instructors now engaged in online teaching, the profession still suffers from a paucity of solid research-based publications. This is disconcerting, especially when we note the sudden emergence of so many new "experts" in online education who, though now enthusiastically engaged in distance teaching, may have never read a single published piece that provides any research-focused foundation for their new role.

Other literature, again in Goodyear's terms, "is suffused with material produced by innovative practitioners, whose enthusiasm is catching, but whose shareable insights are limited by the constraints of everyday language" (2009: vii). We seek to address Goodyear's criticism by offering a book which is informed by a broad range of conceptual and theoretical considerations and insights.

This book, whilst having an overall conceptual frame through which it seeks to capture the key issues and leading debates in the field, has been written in a way that individual chapters stand on their own and need not be read sequentially. The book is aimed mainly at university teachers of all disciplines teaching across a wide range of courses and levels as well as learning technologists who support them. It is deliberately not focused on technology but, instead, on learning and teaching and on contextual issues that impact on them. The book is also aimed at researchers and research students in the field in so far as it attempts an overview and analytical examination of the most significant theoretical sub-domains that have emerged within the field or discipline of e-learning.

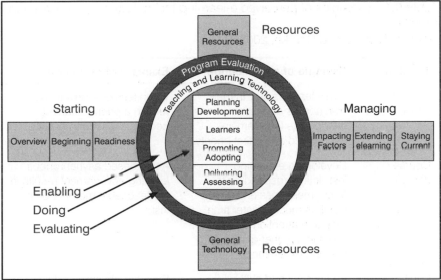

Figure 0.3   The "Whole Picture of e-Learning" model
Source: George Siemens, http://www.elearnspace.org/Articles/
wholepicture.htm

Rather than providing a comprehensive planning tool, of which numerous exist (see e.g. Figure 0.3), we seek to foster critical reflection by providing an overview of some of the key conceptual and theoretical considerations.

The book does not set out to offer a comprehensive literature review; instead, it attempts a guided tour through some seminal material at the interface of theory and practice. "E-learning" has been discussed in the literature for a number of decades now (see e.g. Kanuka and Rourke, 2008; Ravenscroft, 2001) and much can be learnt from what has been written for and against e-learning technologies. Kanuka and Rourke (2008: 6), for example, note that because technologies are designed to serve specific purposes—they call this intentionality—it amplifies those aspects of use— they call this selectivity. Yet, at the same time, they argue, technologies unavoidably reduce other aspects of our experience. See also our brief discussion of affordances in Chapter 5. In their study of experiences of a small number of e-learning practitioners (administrators, teachers, researchers), they identified four themes: flexibility and convenience, course design, equity and equality and thinking and learning skills. Table 0.1 is the summary of amplifications and reductions identified by Kanuka and Rourke (2008: 9) in their research. It is included here by way of exemplification of why a reflective and principled approach to e-learning is required.

Table 0.1 Examples of perceived e-learning technology amplification and reductions

Source: Kanuka and Rourke, 2008: 9

Themes	Example of amplification	Example of reduction
Flexibility, convenience	When learners stay in their own homes and communities, their private lives remain unchanged and a first priority.	When learners' private lives remain a priority, learning becomes a second priority.
Course design	Developing e-learning instruction, responding to forum messages and emails requires much greater time, care and attention and can result in a higher-quality learning experience.	A text-based asynchronous learning environment results in the teachable moment being lost.
Equity, equality	As physical and cultural characteristics are not visible, there is a more equal and equitable platform for communicating.	Because physical and cultural characteristics are not visible, students are not forced to confront their biases.
Thinking, learning skills	Technology is a catalyst for more interactive and meaningful learning activities.	Text-based discussions do not develop verbal skills.

Kanuka and Rourke (2008: 13–14) draw the following conclusions:

- E-learning technology provides opportunities for improved access through the removal of temporal, geographical and situational barriers. But students' coursework is subordinated to other immediate responsibilities, and both students and instructors may experience a loss of a sense of belongingness and awareness of boundaries. ...
- E-learning technology can increase the quality of course design and cost-effectiveness. But it can also result in a loss of cultural discourse, teachable moments, campus culture, academic freedom and teaching as a scholarly activity. ...
- E-learning technology can provide an equitable and equalizing environment. But students are not forced to confront their biases and prejudices.
- E-learning technology has the potential to facilitate higher order learning with text-based asynchronous communication technologies. But opportunities to develop extemporaneous oracy skills are lost.

These are important insights on the basis of which interventions can be formulated.

At the same time, we would argue that there is still some way to go before we fully understand the complex interplay between learning, teaching and technology and that a concerted effort is needed to strengthen our evidence base. This belief is motivated *inter alia* by our own work on e-learning as perceived by students (see e.g. Daly and Pachler, 2007; Daly, Pachler and Lambert, 2004; Daly, Pachler and Pickering, 2003; Daly et al., 2007; Pachler and Daly, 2006a, 2006b; Pickering, Daly and Pachler, 2007) as well as by mobile, portable and ubiquitous technologies coming onto the scene, which this book deliberately excludes. Readers interested in these technologies should see, for example, Pachler, 2007; Pachler, Bachmair and Cook, 2010; Pachler, Pimmer and Seipold, 2010; Vavoula, Pachler and Kukulska-Hulme, 2009.

The book has deliberately been kept manageable in size. Whilst it attempts to cover the most significant trends in the field, it is not possible to provide a fully comprehensive coverage of issues here. The stance taken by us as authors is significantly informed by our own work as tutors, designers and researchers of online university-level provision, predominantly in the field of professional learning.

In Chapter 1, "The 'e' in e-Learning", we explore a range of terms such as e-learning, online learning, blended learning and their relationships with each other as well their definition before we ask the more fundamental question how learning itself best be understood. In addition, we offer a discussion of a "theory" of/for e-learning. Consideration is also briefly given to some policy drivers for e-learning as well as a general discussion about the potential and benefits of technology in (higher) education.

Chapter 2, "Changing Contexts" explores the key contexts affecting e-learning. It discusses how technologies are increasingly blurring the boundaries between formal and informal learning opportunities as well as how learning practices are comprised of multiple processes and are located within technological, social, economic, personal and political contexts. These contexts, it is argued, are interrelated, and they affect how individuals are able to live, work and learn. The chapter presents an "ecological" view of e-learning to explain the relationship between teachers, learners and the environment.

Chapter 3, "Theories, Concepts and Models", examines the ways in which e-learning has led to a range of ways of theoretical and conceptual thinking about altered relations between individuals and the social context, their roles in knowledge construction and the dissemination and distribution of knowledge. Much of the emergent theory sees learning as "a process of restructuring a socially-organized activity" (Koschmann, 2003: 263) and as a combination of individual-cognitive and social-interactionist processes, that is, as essentially *interdependent*.

Chapter 4, "Online Learning and Teaching and Learning about Online Teaching", revisits and expands on the theoretical discussion of learning in Chapter 1 with particular focus on discussing knowledge construction through interaction, participation and distributed cognition. An exploration of the importance of a sense of place in e-learning is followed by a detailed exploration of pedagogical templates, models and frameworks from the literature.

Chapter 5, "e-Assessment, e-Portfolios, Quality Assurance and the Student Experience", pursues issues raised in Chapter 4 and, as its title suggests, gives consideration to issues around the assurance of quality of learning and teaching in e-learning contexts as well as the assessment of learning outcomes including some practical examples. Finally, consideration is given to e-portfolios as tools for supporting and assessing e-learning.

Chapter 6, "Researching e-Learning", starts from the premise that e-learning has many of the attributes of an established research field, maybe with the exception of many of the researchers having migrated to e-learning research from other academic disciplines rather than being "native" to it. One of its key characteristics, the chapter argues, is its "messiness" which makes the need for coherent frameworks for conceptualizing e-learning research all the more important. Following a critical review of some the more prevalent research frameworks the chapter concludes that the relationship between teaching, evaluation and research is in need of fundamental review if research is to make the necessary *difference* to e-learning experiences and argues that a different conceptualization is needed so that practitioners and researchers have roles as co-constructors of the body of knowledge about e-learning.

Notes

1 http://www.timeshighereducation.co.uk/storyasp?storycode=40 6838.
2 http://www.wlecentre.ac.uk.

The "e" in e-Learning 1

Chapter Outline

What do we mean by "e-learning"?   11
What is learning?   17
Towards a theory of/for e-learning   18
Policy as a driver for e-learning   19
Potentials and benefits of technology in education   21
What do we mean by e-learning? Revisited   25
Some theoretical considerations   25
The importance of self-regulation and meta-learning   28
e-Learning 2.0?   32
Some additional theoretical considerations   33
Conclusion   35

What do we mean by "e-learning"?

Definitions of "e-learning" abound, with the letter "e" normally standing for "electronic". Often, e-learning is used synonymously with the term "online learning", that is the emphasis tends to be on learning that takes place at a distance from formal classrooms and is facilitated and supported by web-based technologies. One key aspect in the debate about definitions of the term appears to be around the extent to which specific pedagogical approaches need to be designed into the use of digital technologies.

Yet, an agreed definition of the term e-learning remains strangely elusive. In the commercial world, e-learning is often synonymous with computer-based training (CBT) and web-based training (WBT), that is, the delivery of training material and courses, whereas in university contexts the term tends to relate to a mode of study, which does not require physical presence on campus.

The terms e-learning and online learning can be seen to overlap with other terms such as distance learning, often associated with earlier technologies.

Another term that is frequently used, is "blended learning". It tends to refer to practices in which computer-based activities are integrated with face-to-face (f2f) activities. Garrison and Kanuka (2004: 96) refer to it as "convergence of text-based asynchronous internet-based learning with face-to-face approaches". It is, therefore, a hybrid form of e-learning in which web-based resources are used to supplement or enhance f2f teaching. According to Garrison and Kanuka (p. 97), blended learning represents a fundamental reconceptualization and reorganization of the teaching and learning dynamic starting with various specific contextual needs and contingencies such as disciplinarity, developmental level and resources, be they financial, human and/or technical. As such it creates design challenges.

Kerres and deWitt (2003: 102) point out that blended learning can mean different things to different people; a combination of: different web-based technologies, different pedagogical approaches; any form of instructional technology with f2f instruction; and instructional technology with actual job tasks. According to these authors a survey in 2003 showed that the most widely used "ingredients" of blended learning at the time included: classroom instruction, interactive web-based training, e-mail based communication, self-paced content, threaded discussion, collaborative software, virtual classrooms, print-based workbooks and online testing. With the emergence of social software, a survey conducted today would no doubt produce rather different results.

Oliver and Trigwell (2005) do not find the notion of "blended" learning appealing. For one, they bemoan the fact that the term remains ill-defined. With reference to Whitelock and Jelfs (2003), they note the following three definitions (p. 17):

- the integrated combination of traditional learning with web-based online approaches
- the combination of media and tools employed in an e-learning environment
- the combination of a number of pedagogical approaches, irrespective of learning technology use.

As a result of this array of definitions, Oliver and Trigwell note, almost anything can be viewed as "blended" learning (2005: 18). This, they argue is akin to the stance taken by the UK ministry responsible for education in 2003 when e-learning was defined in a way that anything that had any connection with computers could count as e-learning (see DfES, 2003). As a result of their discussion, Oliver and Trigwell argue for a rebuilding of the concept of blended learning from a grounding in learning theory (2005: 24). They make specific reference to so-called variation theory, which is based on the idea that, for learning to occur, variation must be experienced by the learner as without variation there is no discernment and without discernment there is no learning (p. 22). According to Oliver and Trigwell, such a reinterpretation shifts the emphasis from teacher to learner, from content to experience and from naively conceptualized technologies to pedagogy (p. 24). What is needed, they argue, is a shift away from "manipulating the blend as seen by the teacher, to an in-depth analysis of the variation in the experience of the learning of the student in the blended learning context" (p. 24). Whilst we will not pursue the avenue of variation theory in this book, we agree with Oliver and Trigwell insofar as we too wish to stress the importance of a critical engagement with learning theory in the context of e-learning, however defined.

Given its potential to disrupt traditional structures, pedagogies and operational dynamics, Garrison and Kanuka (2004: 102–3) argue that the successful adoption of a blended learning approach to enhance the effectiveness and efficacy of teaching and learning requires the following:

- creation of clear institutional direction and policy
- frame the potential, increase awareness, and commit
- establishment of a single point of support, quality assurance and project management
- creation of an innovation fund to provide the financial support and incentives to faculty and departments to initiate blended learning course transformations
- investment in establishing a reliable and accessible, technology infrastructure
- strategic selection of prototype projects that prove to be exceptionally successful exemplars of effective learning
- development of formal instructional design support available through a blended format
- systematic evaluation of satisfaction and success of the teaching, learning, technology and administration of new course
- creation of a task group to address issues, challenges and opportunities as well as communicate and recommend new directions to the university community.

Another term frequently used is "mixed-mode", which tends to describe a mixture of online and f2f activities without there necessarily being a great emphasis on or sophisticated use of technology (see e.g. the MTeach in Chapter 4 below).

Jones and Dirckinck-Holmfeld (2009) introduce yet another term, namely "networked" learning by which, following Goodyear et. al. (2004: 1), they understand "learning in which information and communication technology ... is used to promote connections: between one learner and other learners, between learners and tutors; between a learning community and its learning resources".

The question arises what, if any, difference exists between e-learning and mobile learning? Again, the differences are not at all clear-cut in the literature and a range of opinions exists. It can be argued that there are two distinctive differences: one is the portability of mobile devices compared with other tools such as personal computers and, to a lesser extent, portable computers, which are often the main device used for e-learning; the other concerns personal ownership of devices and their embeddedness in the everyday life-worlds and media habits of learners. The revised HEFCE (Higher Education Funding Council for England) e-learning strategy (HEFCE and JISC, 2005: 6) stresses the need for institutions to facilitate the use of their own devices in institutional contexts, and to personalize institutional services to meet the requirements of learners. Therefore, given their relatively small size, mobile devices—despite some inherent limitations, certainly in the past, for example around text input and representation due to size of keyboard and screen—are more readily available in a wide range of situations, and learners tend to be more intimately familiar with their functionalities and are more likely to have personalized them in line with their preferences and use habits. With mobile devices becoming ever more powerful computational devices and in view of predictions for the coming years for ubiquitous computing and for mobile phones to become the prime means of accessing the internet (see e.g. de Waale, 2010) the distinction between e-learning and mobile learning is likely to become increasingly artificial and the more generic term technology-enhanced learning, that is, the support of learning through technology, might, therefore, be conceptually more durable.

JISC (Joint Information Systems Committee), an influential body in the UK supporting higher education institutions in the implementation of new technologies, for example, by providing guidance or funding research and software development as well as providing technological infrastructure such as high-speed internet connectivity, defined e-learning as "enhanced learning". In two publications, one in 2004 and the other more recently in 2009, it sets out what might be meant by e-learning.

What is e-learning?

Defined as "learning facilitated and supported through the use of information and communications technology", e-learning may involve the use of some, or all, of the following technologies:

- desktop and laptop computers
- software, including assistive software
- interactive whiteboards
- digital cameras
- mobile and wireless tools, including mobile phones
- electronic communication tools, including email, discussion boards, chat facilities and video conferencing
- Virtual Learning Environments (VLEs)
- learning activity management systems

E-learning can cover a spectrum of activities from supporting learning, to blended learning (the combination of traditional and e-learning practices), to learning that is delivered entirely online. Whatever the technology, however, learning is the vital element. e-Learning is no longer simply associated with distance or remote learning, but forms part of a conscious choice of the best and most appropriate ways of promoting effective learning.

Figure 1.1   e-Learning = enhanced learning
Source: JISC, 2004: 10

Figures 1.1 and 1.2 show that the story of e-learning in the so-called "noughties" is one of evolution rather than of revolution, that is, "changes in the practices of things with which we are already familiar, the incorporation of the new within existing frameworks ... and a shift in ways of understanding that are different from what has gone before but are inextricably linked to it" (Daly and Pachler, 2010: 218). Figure 1.1 supports the earlier argument about the use of the term "technology-enhanced learning" in favour of e-learning.

"e-Learning" is still widely used to refer to the application of technology to learning. However, the term "technology-enhanced learning" is gaining favour since it emphasizes how technology adds value to learning by enabling:

- connectivity to information and to others
- 24/7 access to learning resources
- greater choice over the time, place and pace of study
- alternative modes of study: distance, blended work-based, partially or wholly campus-based
- knowledge-sharing and co-authoring across multiple locations
- opportunities for reflection and planning in personal learning spaces
- rapid feedback on formative assessments
- more active learning by means of interactive technologies and multimedia resources
- participation in communities of knowledge, inquiry and learning
- learning by discovery in virtual worlds
- development of skills for living and working in a digital age

Figure 1.2 e-Learning = enhanced learning
Source: JISC, 2007: 10

Importantly, the documents foreground the need for an understanding of pedagogy—defined as "the activities of education, or instructing or teaching" and as "activities that impart knowledge or skill" (JISC, 2004: 10). In relation to the transformational potential of technology in terms of teaching and learning, Kirkwood (2009: 110) notes that some US studies found that teachers' use of technologies tended to maintain rather than alter existing classroom practices due to certain contextual factors, in particular variations in users' conceptions of teaching and learning and the backwash effect of assessment requirements. According to Kirkwood the situation is often made worse by technology-focused polices and strategies.

As Kress and Pachler (2007: 16) note, currently prefixes for the word "learning" abound, among them a number referring to technology: in addition to e-learning, there is m- or mobile learning, u- or ubiquitous learning, online learning, virtual learning and so on. This proliferation of descriptors raises the question of whether they do, indeed, point to different kinds of learning. A closer examination suggests that, rather than denoting different "kinds" of learning, they refer to differences in conditions and environments of learning. Are the differences in conditions and environments denoted so great that they result in significant differences in the experience and processes of learning? Our answer to this question is "No." In order to substantiate this answer, it is necessary to explore the question "what is learning?"

What is learning?

Research by Säljö (1979) reported by Kirkwood (2009: 110–12) delineates a number of distinct conceptions of learning by students:

- learning as the increase in knowledge
- learning as memorization
- learning as the acquisition of facts, procedures and so on, that can be retained and/or utilized in practice
- learning as the abstraction of meaning
- learning as an interpretive process aimed at the understanding of reality

In addition to the differences in conceptions of learning across students, according to Perry (1970), also referred to by Kirkwood, conceptions also vary within students according to their stages of intellectual development. Kirkwood goes on to argue that an individual's conception of learning will determine his or her expectations of, and approaches to, learning, for example in terms of surface-level (memorization and reproduction) or deep-level (developing and extending meaning and understanding) processing.

For the purposes of this book, we understand learning as the twin processes of "coming to know" and "being able to operate" successfully in and across new and ever-changing contexts and learning spaces, as a process of meaning-making through communication and as an augmentation of inner, conceptual, and outer, semiotic resources (see also Pachler, Bachmair and Cook, 2010; Kress and Pachler, 2007).

Similar differences in conceptions of learning and teaching and the nature of knowledge exist on the part of teachers.

We will examine the pedagogical implications in Chapters 4 and 5 on teaching, learning and assessment.

Towards a theory of/for e-learning

Theories of e-learning are not distinct from theories of learning generally. Theoretical explanations of technology-assisted learning are concerned with the contribution of environments, tools and modes of communicating to the social and individual resources that people draw on to constitute and share ideas. Nichols (2003) has argued that the lack of established theory in e-learning can be seen to hinder further development in e-learning. In a bid to help establish a theory for e-learning, he posits 10 hypotheses (he views hypotheses "that apply to all instances of a particular phenomenon" (p. 1) as constituent parts of theory):

H1   E-learning is a means of implementing education that can be applied within varying education models (e.g. f2f or distance education) and educational philosophies (e.g. behaviourism and constructivism).

H2   E-learning enables unique forms of education that fit within the existing paradigms of f2f and distance education.

H3   The choice of e-learning tools should reflect rather than determine the pedagogy of a course; how technology is used is more important than which technology is used.

H4   E-learning advances primarily through the successful implementation of pedagogical innovation.

H5   E-learning can be used in two major ways: the presentation of education content and the facilitation of education processes.

H6   E-learning tools are best made to operate within a carefully selected and optimally integrated course design model.

H7   E-learning tools and techniques should be used only after consideration has been given to online vs. offline trade-offs.

H8   Effective e-learning practice considers the ways in which end-users will engage with the learning opportunities provided to them.

H9   The overall aim of education, that is, the development of the learner in the context of a predetermined curriculum or set of learning objectives, does not change when e-learning is applied.

H10 Only pedagogical advantages will provide a lasting rationale for implementing e-learning approaches.

With the help of such hypotheses, Nichols argues, a yardstick for the evaluation of practice can be provided which counters the lack of established theory. He also sees them addressing the inherent lack of transferability in the majority of the literature about e-learning, certainly at the time Nichols' piece was written, owing to an approach characterized by him thus: "here's what we did and here's the evaluation" (2003: 1).

Whilst clearly helpful in setting out broad parameters for the field (e.g. H3 "how technology is used is more important than which technology is used" gives clear guidance about the relative importance of pedagogy over technology), the level of generality of the hypotheses limits their analytical "purchase" for the purpose of planning interventions or evaluating practice. For this reason, we will provide a critical overview of prevalent theories of e-learning in Chapter 3. Here we simply wish to reiterate a point made by Anderson (2008: 45) that theory allows us, and forces us, to see the big picture and allows us to take a broader perspective on our practice, which helps us relate what we do to the work of others and, thereby, hopefully contributes to synergies, coherence and a deeper understanding as well as supports the transfer of experiences across contexts.

Policy as a driver for e-learning

The popularity of e-learning is usually associated with its (perceived) benefits around fitting in with learners' time requirements (any time), with overcoming problems around geographical distance (any place) or with offering increased flexibility (e.g. just for me or just in time), and thereby improving access and increasing convenience. According to Allen and Seamen (2008), around a quarter of all students in post-secondary education in the USA were taking fully online courses in 2008 with a report by Ambient Insight Research (2009) noting the figure rises to 44 per cent when taking into account blended provision. It seems legitimate to assume a similar degree of "penetration" of the education "market" by e-learning in the UK. Certainly, the responsible ministry and the HEFCE has promoted the use of technology to enhance teaching and learning for a number of years now. This includes the DfES (Department for Education and Skills) Harnessing Technology strategy (see DfES 2005; Becta 2009) aimed at transforming learning and children's services. It also includes HEFCE's strategy for e-learning in 2005 (revised in 2009). And it includes HEFCE's extensive Centre for Excellence in Teaching and Learning (CETL) programme from 2005 to

2010, which has also tended to focus, at least in part, on pedagogical innovation through technology. Similarly Becta, for the school and further education sector, and JISC, for the higher education sector, have been supporting educational institutions in the innovative use of digital technologies inter alia, with the aim of enhancing and transforming teaching and learning to improve outcomes for learners, accessibility of information and services, efficiency and effectiveness as well as to engage hard to reach learners (see DfES, 2005: 4; HEFCE, 2009: 2).

The HEFCE (2009: 12–15) suggests the following framework as part of their strategy for e-learning. It includes seven areas of activity against which they list numerous strategic priorities for HEIs to consider in their planning for, and implementation of, e-learning at institutional level:

Table 1.1   Seven areas of e-learning activity

Activity area	Strategic priorities
Pedagogy, curriculum design and development	Enhancing excellence and innovation in teaching and learning Enhancing flexibility and choice for learners Enhancing student achievement Improving employability and skills Attracting and retaining learners Supporting research-based or enquiry-based learning Engaging employers (or other stakeholders) in curriculum design and delivery Improving efficiency of curriculum design and delivery processes
Learning resources and environments	Enhancing flexibility and choice for learners Enhancing student achievement Improving employability and skills Widening participation and improving access Effective management of learning resources Designing and maintaining effective environments for learning
Lifelong learning processes and practices	Improving employability and skills Enhancing flexibility and choice for learners Widening participation and improving access to learning opportunities Supporting diverse learners' needs Retaining learners and meeting learners' expectations Co-operating with other institutions, colleges and campuses

Strategic management, human resources and capacity development	Enhancing excellence in teaching Enhancing excellence in research Workforce development Business/community links Improving efficiency and effectiveness of institutional processes
Quality	Institutional quality processes can support objectives and enhance benefits in all the other areas
Research and evaluation	Enhancing excellence in learning and teaching Enhancing excellence in research Enhancing understanding of learning and teaching processes Enhancing institutional processes (especially quality assurance and review)
Infrastructure and technical standards	Enhancing flexibility for learners Supporting diverse learners' needs Enhancing efficiency of institutional processes Enhancing the technical infrastructure Enhancing the information environment Ensuring effective ICT investments and effective use of existing ICT resources Sustainability ("green" computing)

The reasons for the adoption of e-learning, therefore, are manifold and span across all aspects and dimensions of higher education activity.

Potentials and benefits of technology in education

Krämer and Schmidt (2001: 195) delineate the potential of technology in education and learning as follows:

- The same content can be presented using different media types including text, two- and three-dimensional graphics, sound, image sequences or simulations.
- Different perspectives and accesses to the same topic can be used to provide cognitive flexibility.
- Different media are synchronized into multi-modal presentations.
- Multimedia components can be networked to hypermedia learning applications according to logic, didactic or other meaningful relationships among components.

- Different customized "tours" can be superimposed on a web of learning components with a view to maximizing re-use and adapting existing contents to new courses and curricula.
- Educational software development and knowledge modelling tools facilitate authoring of multimedia educational material and technology.
- Flexible navigation control lets learners explore a networked information space at their own pace and orientation. But it can also provide rigid guidance including conditional selection of follow-on information and progress on successful completion of given learning tasks.
- Interaction facilities provide learners with opportunities for experimentation, context-dependent feedback, and constructive problem solving.
- Asynchronous and synchronous communication and collaboration facilities help to bridge geographical distance between course providers, teachers and students.
- Virtual laboratories and environments can be used to offer near authentic work situations, opportunities for hands-on experimentation and constructive problem solving.
- Operation sequences and preferred learning paths can be recorded, evaluated and reactivated if necessary. The students can add their own reference structures and personal notes to the course material.

Whilst they stress—and we would agree—that the role of technology in education is sometimes (if not often) exaggerated, their judicious and pedagogically principled use can be seen to yield great potential. It goes without saying that—given this array of possibilities—the extent to which they are being harnessed varies. Indeed, research also shows that the extent to which teachers and learners used and value them is also highly variable (Kirkwood, 2009: 109).

One important driver for e-learning, in particular at a meso- and macro-policy-level has been the belief in its ability to bring about increased productivity and performance. At a macro-level, for example, policy initiatives around lifelong learning and widening participation have seen e-learning as an integral mechanism of enabling an ever increasing number of people to access learning and to do so throughout their lifespan. At a meso-level, institutions have seen e-learning as a possible means of coping with a reduction in funding levels as well as an opportunity for broadening their catchment area for students beyond local, regional and even national boundaries. A recent meta-analysis of research published by the US Department of Education (Means et al., 2009) explored the question of the relative efficacy of online and f2f instruction. Based on a review of studies of web-based instruction with a random-assignment or controlled quasi-experimental design and examining only effects for objective measures of student learning, as well as bearing in mind that only few such rigorous research studies have been published, the study concluded that:

- Students who took all or part of their class online performed better, on average, than those taking the same course through traditional f2f instruction (p. xiv).
- Instruction combining online and f2f elements had a larger advantage relative to purely f2f instruction than did purely online instruction.
- Studies in which learners in the online condition spent more time on tasks than students in the f2f condition found a greater benefit for online learning.
- Most of the variations in the way in which different studies implemented online learning did not affect student learning outcomes significantly.
- The effectiveness of online learning approaches appears quite broad across different content and learner types (p. xv).
- Effect sizes were larger for studies in which the online and f2f conditions varied in terms of curriculum materials and aspects of instructional approach in addition to the medium of instruction.
- Blended and purely online learning conditions implemented within a single study generally result in similar student learning outcomes.
- Elements such as video or online quizzes do not appear to influence the amount that students learn in online classes.
- Online learning can be enhanced by giving learners control of their interactions with media and prompting learner reflection.
- Providing guidance for learning for groups of students appears less successful than does using such mechanisms with individual learners (p. xvi).

The question about the tangible benefits of e-learning is clearly also of relevance to UK policy makers given the significant levels of investment made in e-learning in recent years. A recent project report (JISC, 2008b) explores the issue of what kinds of evidence can be provided in support of tangible benefits of e-learning. The most commonly cited types of evidence, according to the report (p. 6), were: exam results, internal and external evaluations, student feedback and focus groups, system logs, departmental budgets and anecdotal evidence from both students and staff. The types of tangible benefits evidenced are presented under the following headings (p. 7):

- effect on learning (e.g. context, style, insight and reflective practice)
- effect on exam results
- effect on student personal development (e.g. skills, employability, confidence)
- student satisfaction with e-learning (e.g. effect on motivation, attendance and enjoyment, as shown in national survey, institutional survey, module evaluation, focus groups or other)
- innovation in teaching, learning and assessment (e.g. stimulus to creative approaches)
- influence on educational research
- staff satisfaction with e-learning
- effect on staff personal development (e.g. skills, employability, confidence)
- influence on recruitment (students or staff: e.g. through greater accessibility, opening up new markets)
- influence on retention (e.g. students or staff)
- influence on policy (e.g. institutional, faculty/school, departmental or other extra-institutional body)
- effect on resources (e.g. effect on cost of delivery, time, applying full economic costing to teaching and learning)
- modifications to learning spaces (e.g. libraries, wireless networks, informal learning spaces)
- effect on management of learning assets (e.g. institutional IP, repositories)
- effect on a social justice agenda (e.g. widening participation, provision of space for consideration of differing or challenging perspectives).

This list shows that, in addition to "hard" statistical measures, seemingly in the forefront of the US study, softer, less easily quantifiable measures, are rather prominent in the JISC report and that it is important to explore the notion of benefit from the perspective of a wide range of stakeholders. As a consequence, the benefits of e-learning are not presented in terms of hard-and-fast facts in the document, but instead in the form of situated case studies under the headings cost savings/resource efficiency, recruitment and retention, skills and employability, student achievement, inclusion as well as widening participation and social equity.

In his review of evidence from research and evaluation studies Kirkwood (2009) sounds a salutary note about e-learning achieving the anticipated transformations in learning and teaching. He stresses the fact that technologies, in themselves, do not result in improved educational outcomes and ways of working, that contextual factors are of greater significance in determining how and why e-learning is used and that both teachers and learners need to understand why e-learning is used and the rewards they expect to gain (p. 107).

What do we mean by e-learning? Revisited

In an earlier publication (Daly and Pachler, 2010), we offered the following definition of e-learning:

> A set of practices which enhance the potential of people to learn with others via technology-aided interaction, in contexts which can be "free" of barriers of time and place. It involves the utilisation of a range of digital resources—visual, auditory and text-based—which enable learners to access, create and publish material which serves educational purposes. ... this material can be shared electronically with fellow learners and teachers both within and beyond the bounds of formal education contexts (p. 217).

Such a view of e-learning, therefore, foregrounds what people do with technology, rather than technology itself, and, at the same time, it is based around an understanding of learning as a process of meaning-making through communication around digital artefacts.

Some theoretical considerations

We draw on our understanding of the seminal work of Diana Laurillard's discursive "conversational framework" model, which describes interrelationships between, and activities by, teachers and learners in the meaning-making process. Ostensibly, Laurillard

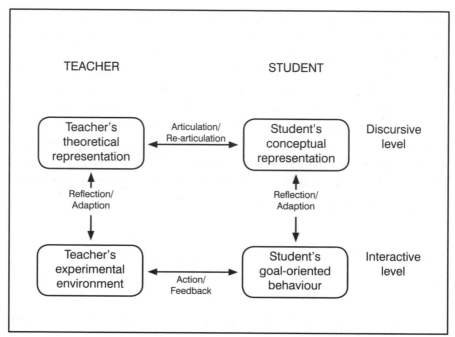

Figure 1.3 The conversational framework for the learning process
Source: Laurillard et al., 2000

(2002) explains the learning process as being akin to a "conversation" between the teacher and the student that operates at a discursive and interactive level linked by reflection and adaptation (see Figures 1.3, 1.4).

The model can be seen to be based on a dialectic cycle of theorizing, design and evaluation. Learning is seen as a series of iterative conversations: with the external world and its artefacts, with oneself and also with other learners and teachers. Learning is most successful, it is argued, when the learner is in control of the activity, able to test ideas by performing experiments, ask questions, collaborate with other people, seek out new knowledge, and plan new actions.

Pachler, Bachmair and Cook (2010) argue that the notion of conversation, foregrounds the link to people at the expense of links to systems and media structures and we ask whether the term communication may better express these. Indeed, Pachler, Bachmair and Cook (2010: 25; see also Pachler, 2010) propose a socio-cultural ecological model comprising of agency, cultural practices and structures to enable an analytical engagement around educational uses of (mobile) learning technologies:

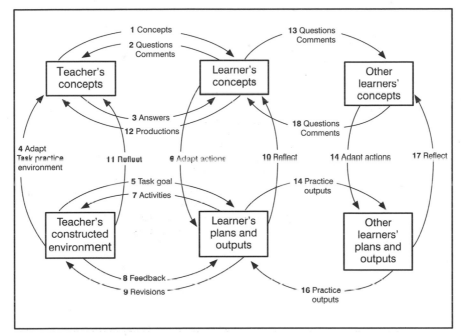

Figure 1.4   The conversational framework for supporting the formal learning process
Source: Laurillard 2007: 160

- Agency: young people can be seen to increasingly display a new habitus of learning, in which they constantly see their life-worlds framed both as a challenge and as an environment and a potential resource for learning, in which their expertise is individually appropriated in relation to personal definitions of relevance and in which the world has become the curriculum populated by mobile device users in a constant state of expectancy and contingency.
- Cultural practices: mobile devices are increasingly used for social interaction, communication and sharing; learning is viewed as culturally situated meaning-making inside and outside of educational institutions and media use in everyday life have achieved cultural significance.
- Structures: young people increasingly live in a society of individualized risks, new social stratifications, individualized mobile mass communication and highly complex and proliferated technological infrastructure; their learning is significantly governed by the curricular frames of educational institutions with specific approaches towards the use of new cultural resources for learning. (Pachler, 2010: 158)

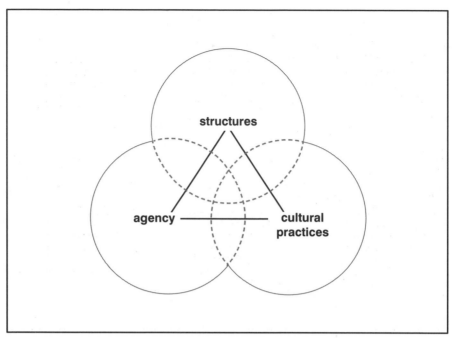

Figure 1.5   Key components of a socio-cultural ecological approach
Source: http://www.londonmobilelearning.net

Although this model was developed specifically for mobile technologies, in particular convergent smartphones, it can be seen to apply equally to e-learning. In e-learning, as in mobile learning, the agency of the learner can be seen to be key given the relative lack of teacher intervention, be it in setting up and framing learning activities and tasks, guiding learners through them, supporting them with modelling and scaffolding and so on. And it is framed by the cultural practices of everyday life as well as of schools, universities and the work place whilst at the same time being situated in the characteristics of their social environment and milieu as well as the affordances of the technological infrastructure available to them.

The importance of self-regulation and meta-learning

One important issue relating to the importance of learner agency in the context of e-learning is that of self-regulation. From the literature on assessment for learning and formative (e-)assessment (see e.g. Pachler et al., 2009) we know that self-regulation, and how it links to motivation and emotional factors, must be considered to be a crucial aspect of learning: "the extent to which learners are capable of regulating their own learning greatly enhances their learning outcomes" (Steffens, 2006: 353).

According to the literature, self-regulation can be seen to involve several components, namely cognitive, affective, motivational and behavioural. That means self-regulation assumes active participation of learners on those levels in their own learning. In many models the process involved is described as being cyclic involving goal setting, monitoring process and strategies, feedback and self-evaluation (Steffens, 2006: 354).

Banyard, Underwood and Twiner (2006: 475), rightly in our view, note that self-regulated learning requires greater effort from the learner and posit three features of motivational belief: self-efficacy, task value beliefs and mastery goal orientation. In the context of e-learning these features require careful consideration at the design stage as well as in terms of learner support.

From research we conducted with our students enrolled on a mixed-mode professional Masters level course we know (see Daly et al., 2007) that the subjective, perceptual and experiential aspects of being an e-learner are extremely important, particularly in the context of professional development contexts. Tensions can easily exist with learners' perception of themselves as competent, skilled professionals which can lead to unsettling and destabilizing e-learning experiences involving disorientation and reorientation. Our research shows that e-learning can be an uncertain, even painful experience for learners particularly concerning learners' conceptions of what e-learning will be like compared with their personal learning histories. In our work learners were mostly unprepared for any significant epistemological challenges to their understanding of learning and knowledge brought about by engaging in collaborative e-learning practices. A sub-textual analysis of our data identified the themes in Figure 1.6.

Experiences within any of those spectrums could be multiple and oppositional with conflicting experiences potentially co-existing within the same person and across a group of learners. It is important to note that progression in learners' positions over time is not necessarily linear and there is no hierarchy of experiences and accomplishments. For the majority of our students the persistent and recurring experiences were of being in transition between states and processes with varying degrees of familiarity, both socially and intellectually. The transitions were partly to do with adjusting to new ways of establishing social relations

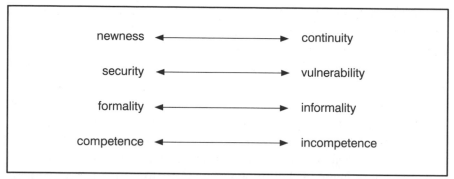

Figure 1.6 Themes of transition in e-learning experiences
Source: http://www.wlecentre.ac.uk/cms/files/projects/reports/PR_Daly-Pachler-Pickering-Bezemer_2006.pdf

in a collaborative online context and, related to this, to do with learning how to learn. By creating the communicative context for themselves, participants developed knowledge about how to "be" a learner in this situation, making collective and individual sense of the initial "online limbo" at the same time as engaging with the course curriculum. Such activity affords a potentially high degree of agency to the learner, whose actions and interactions shape what things mean and bring into being new conceptions of the self-as-learner as an individual in relation to others. Engagement in collaborative e-learning makes demands of learners that have important potential for re-evaluation of the self-as-learner. However, learners need to feel that it is worth investing as a person in the context-making processes that are a prerequisite. Our data suggest that such context-making processes take time and involve risk-taking but have the potential to bring benefits for the learners, manifested in a variety of types of meta-level activity.

Related to this is work by Hughes (2009: 295) on identity congruence between individuals and groups which distinguishes three distinct but interrelated aspects:

> Firstly, there is the personal level of identification with peers ... social identity congruence. Secondly, there is identification with the processes, practices and technologies of social learning or operational identity congruence. Thirdly, identification with the ideas, concepts and knowledges that are under construction gives knowledge-related identity congruence.

In short, learning online is a highly complex and potentially emotionally fraught undertaking. This is borne out by the data in our study (Daly et al., 2007) of e-learning. "Katy" is a case study which presents evidence of all three forms of "identity congruence" as defined by Hughes (2009).

Case study: Katy

Katy was one of only two people in the group with prior experience of e-learning. This and her commitment to rigorously logico-scientific forms of knowledge made an impact on her experiences and were a main source of reflection and conflict regarding "identity congruence". She stated in an interview "I love online stuff because I'm totally used to it". The technological issues, which are a source of initial anxiety for many of the novices, were not relevant to her and she related how she revels in using the wider affordances of e-learning, "having Google and Wikipedia at my fingertips". At the same time however, she experienced other forms of newness, which unsettled her as the course progresses. As an experienced e-learner she was able to comprehend early on the "newness" of the experience is attributable largely to social relations, which are made online rather than technological issues:

> There's this entirely new social situation. You have no idea what the netiquette is, or what's the expected culture, or that sort of thing. And so everyone sort of was very much kind of sending out these signals and going, "Ah, I don't really know what I'm doing!" … there was quite a lot of sort of general wariness … I think even for those of us who … knew online learning … because it's a new set of online learning, and it's a new community.

Referring to herself as "fairly quiet" in face-to-face situations, Katy claimed that online communication empowered her by affording her more licence to participate and to adopt an assertive persona, becoming a different type of person online, being argumentative and arguing strongly for her positions in ways she would never do in a seminar room: "I tend to be horribly argumentative if I email … in person I tend to be very non-confrontational". Because she valued e-learning as a means of adopting counter-positions, she became dissatisfied with the "courtesy" which some other participants said they valued in online exchange. She regretted that she inadvertently offended another participant by arguing so strongly, and consciously tried to reign in any trace of "nastiness", but she felt that this makes learning less effective for her.

A further internal struggle was coming to terms with the socio-constructivist approaches to learning, which underpin the online discussions: "if we're going to talk about learning, then I want to hear what everybody in the world who is important has ever said about learning, and then maybe I'll have my own opinion". Her scepticism meant that she found it "quite uncomfortable" to be asked to rely on the group discussions as a key source of knowledge-building and wanted to be given "the right answer". Reconciling this scepticism with the course e-learning pedagogy she referred to as "an ongoing journey". She accepted that she held multiple and oppositional opinions about the experience, saying at one point "What's great about the online discussions is that I'm getting what they think about something that someone else has thought", it is "not just discussion, it's a deeper thing".

The case of Katy reaffirms Oliver and Trigwell's (2005) argument that, to understand e-learning, a theoretical focus needs to be on the variation in the experience of the learning brought about by technologies.

e-Learning 2.0?

As a response to the rapid changes in the technology infrastructure with the onset of social software and applications, such as wikis, blogs, social networking, podcasts and virtual worlds, increasingly the term e-learning 2.0 is preferred to e-learning. The continued, and often rapid, changes in the technological structures governing e-learning—some speak of perpetual obsolescence—therefore, mean that evolution is a permanent feature. E-learning 1.0 tends to be associated with the delivery of content, such as readings, to students on the basis of which they prepared assignments, which are assessed by tutors. It is usually associated with so-called virtual learning environments (VLEs), managed learning environments (MLEs) or learning management systems (LMSs), which provide a portal for online learner activity such as asynchronous (delayed-time) or synchronous (real-time) communication. The former harnesses the potential of the new tools and applications for social learning and tends to be grounded in group interaction and online learning communities. Such divisions are not clear-cut. Even relatively early examples of e-learning courses, such as the mixed-mode Master of Teaching offered at the Institute of Education, London since the early 2000s, to the development of which the current authors contributed significantly, were based on principles of computer-mediated communication (CMC), that is, a text-mediational view of learning which "links the concepts of expression, interaction, reflection, problem-solving, critical thinking, and literacy with the various uses of talk, text, inquiry, and collaboration" (Warschauer, 1997: 472; see also e.g. Daly and Pachler, 2007; Daly, Pachler and Pickering, 2003; Daly et al., 2007; Pachler and Daly, 2006a, 2006b).

Some additional theoretical considerations

Ravenscroft (2001: 133) posits that e-learning is not a recent phenomenon. He makes this point because he thinks that we should be mindful of the history of design around technology-enhanced learning in order not simply to replicate or augment "conventional approaches" to teaching and learning but to properly exploit the affordances of contemporary technologies. Like Nichols, he urges us to step back from more practical concerns, at least momentarily, and to consider the more fundamental issues concerning the learning process and interactions supported by technology. For him the focus should be on the interactions technology can stimulate, support and favour that, for him, are linked to conceptual development and improvements in understanding (p. 134).

In his paper he provides an interesting historical overview of learning theories and how they link to the use of technology in teaching and learning. Of particular relevance for Ravenscroft— and we agree with him albeit with some modifications (see e.g. Pachler, Bachmair and Cook, 2010)—is the work of Lev Vygotsky in the field of social constructivism who emphasizes the necessity for collaborative, argumentative and reflective discourses as a central part of the learning process (Ravenscroft, 2001: 141). The interaction between tutors and learners as well as between learners and learners in e-learning operates on the basis of proficient use of sign systems, normally language (written or spoken) and increasingly also images. Such tools, to use Vygotsky's terminology, in this theory need to be "internalised to operate as a mediating factor between environmental stimuli and an individual's response" (Ravenscroft, 2001: 141) in order to bring about the qualitative developmental transition from lower to higher level activity and for us to become conscious and in control of our mental activities (p. 141). Ravenscroft points out that "it is through the communicative process that external sign systems conveying interpersonal communication become internalised to operate as intrapersonal psychological tools that can transform mental functioning" (p. 141). Technology represents a tool that mediates these processes and co-operative dialogue between the teacher, or a more knowledgeable peer, and the learner helps to achieve the "systematicity and logic of adult reasoning" (p. 142). Ravenscroft summarizes the relevance of Vogotsky for e-learning design as follows (pp. 142–3):

> First, learning, and particularly the development of higher mental processes, requires a cooperative interaction between a student and a more learned other, where the latter may be a human tutor or an intelligent computer system.
>
> Secondly, learning is engineered by shifting the learner's zone of proximal development, which can be achieved via a collaborative dialectic maintained between the learner and a tutor or system.
>
> Thirdly, meaning—in the head—derives from the social context and the interaction, so the learner develops a conceptual understanding "through" dialogue. Or, putting it another way, "thought follows action".
>
> Finally, language is considered the primary mediator of thought and a tool for thinking, so the external dialectic processes engaged between interlocutors becomes internalised to provide improved reasoning and reflective capabilities.

These considerations support the focus on CMC as an integral part of e-learning. In Chapters 4 and 5 on teaching, learning and assessment we will consider the operationalization of these ideas. Unlike Ravenscroft we do not promote a computational tutoring approach—his paper goes on to consider intelligent dialogue systems as a possible trajectory for e-learning. Nevertheless, the notion that dialogue has an important role to play in shaping conceptual development is one we consider to be crucial. Important questions remain, however, about what kinds of dialogue and social interaction, group settings and tasks are most effective and how pedagogical intervention ensures that technology is not seen merely as a conduit of discourse but as an effective mediational and constructivist tool.

A related notion is computer-supported collaborative learning (CSCL). It is based on the design of instruction, which requires learners to collaborate on tasks online and, in the process, to construct knowledge. In so doing, it breaks with traditional models of teaching based on the transfer of knowledge from the teacher to the learner who, using her cognitive resources, has to try to make sense of the information provided. In the CSCL paradigm learning is situated in a social context around the use of technological tools for effective collaboration. A more detailed discussion of collaborative knowledge building together with an exploration of questions around mediated, distributed and shared group cognition will follow in the chapters on teaching, learning and assessment.

> How are the individual cognitive processes of participants influenced by social interaction and how does learning take place in the computer-mediated interaction between participants? Do cognitive phenomena exist transpersonally? Can learning be distributed across people and artefacts? (Suthers, 2006: 665)

Conclusion

From this overview of definitional bases and issues concerning e-learning at least one important conclusion can be drawn, namely that, in order to be successful, e-learning interventions need to build on an explicit theory of learning and to foreground pedagogical considerations over technological ones.

Changing Contexts 2

Chapter Outline

Introduction	37
Ecology of learning with technologies	38
Technological developments and changing views of knowledge and learners	40
Socio-cultural practices	43
Policy-making	45
Policy tensions affecting educational institutions	49
Changing personal/public boundaries	51
Challenges for schools, post-16 colleges and universities	54
Conclusion	55

Introduction

In the introduction to this book, we discussed e-learning in a context of rapid societal and technological change. There is a well-established discourse (e.g. Borgman et al., 2008; Johnson et al., 2010) which acknowledges that the rate of change is considerable and that the consequences for learning are significant. In 2002, Synder was telling us that within "the new communications order ... the world for which schools were formed no longer exists" (pp. 173–9). It is, of course, even more apparent now. It is far from the case however, that practices within formal learning institutions like schools, universities and colleges of further education currently reflect this situation, although there are growing examples of significant advances in particular cases (e.g. with regard to the adoption of Web 2.0 pedagogies and infrastructure in some UK universities: Franklin and van Harmelen, 2007). Learning practices are comprised of multiple processes and are a complex reflection of changes in technological, social, economic, personal and political contexts. These contexts are interrelated, and their shifts affect how individuals are able to live, work and learn. E-learning is by no means "ubiquitous" although perhaps we can now say that technologies are, in many parts of the world. We start this chapter on changing contexts by presenting an "ecological" view of e-learning, which is concerned to explain the relationship between teachers, learners and the environment in which they practice and learn. This view looks at the learning environment as a set of processes which are interrelated in complex ways. The environment is made up of a range of social, cultural and technological resources which are not fixed but dynamic. From an ecological perspective, if one aspect of the environment is changed, all of the processes are altered in some way because they are linked with each other, and all elements are affected. When applied to e-learning, this means that it is impossible to focus simply on one element (e.g. individual teachers' skills or a particular technological innovation or learners' experiences) to understand what is going on.

Ecology of learning with technologies

The metaphor of ecology, or natural systems processes whose separate parts are in complex interrelation with each other, has been long-established to describe educational scenarios. Zhao and Frank (2003) argue that the metaphor of an ecosystem emphasizes interaction, complexity and the need to understand systems as wholes rather than as a collection of parts. The advent of technologies has brought additional complexity to the range of processes and factors which need to be understood in order to examine learning and how it is contextualized in contemporary settings. An ecological perspective means that the factors affecting e-learning need to be seen as inter-connected and context-specific.

Davis (2008) argues that an ecological perspective helps us to understand the subtle and shifting balance in relationships between factors, and unique permutations are constantly developing and evolving. For that reason, practitioner development in education institutions depends on many factors. It is important to avoid overemphasis on single-strategy "solutions" to embedding e-learning in formal settings. Overemphasis on some factors can in fact inhibit the growth of, or even "kill off", other potentially beneficial factors, because they upset a balance or over-prescribe the conditions of the environment. A focus, historically, on technology, leaders, innovators, standardization and so on, has not addressed the complexity of practitioners' learning across the sectors and phases of education (see e.g. Daly, Pachler and Pelletier, 2009a; Preston, 2004), which is central to being able to harness technologies effectively in practice and which will be experienced uniquely and variably within even constant external environmental factors. Flexibility, responsiveness, creativity and respect for difference are core ingredients in successful practitioner development. So too is the recognition that the education practitioner is a whole person, whose relationship with the environment is shaped by personal attributes and experiences.

Davis presents an ecological view of how school teachers develop practice which incorporates technologies. Her model can be argued to have wide applicability across educational settings, because it presents how teachers, learners and technologies interact with each other within a set of broader relationships with all of these dimensions. She places the practitioner at the centre of concentric contexts of influence: the classroom, school, wider education district/authority, regional and national factors, all of which are populated by different groups of stakeholders (parents, local and national government organizations, professional groups). Across all these, she identifies four strands of influence on developing practice—political, bureaucratic, professional and commercial.

This view of developing practice does not mean that the teacher (or higher education tutor) is passively positioned within the environment. Hammond et al.'s (2009: 71) findings with student teachers who were "very good" with technologies has wider significance for understanding how all practitioners are constantly "negotiating practice" within environmental factors as they learn how to "do" e-learning.

> Learning to teach, and learning to teach well, can be considered not only as an apprenticeship, a kind of induction into a community of practice, but a more proactive process in which the student teacher is negotiating a practice within an environment which encourages some activities and discourages others. (Hammond et al., 2009: 71)

No matter how skilfully the teacher engages with technologies, it is an understanding of how the learners engage with ideas, culture and experience that will support their learning—and how they need to do this as part of a complex social practice. Personalized learning needs to be treated with caution in this context. Learning is about *being a person* and how the person learns in relation to social and technological contexts—in other words, it is "sociogenic", and our focus is on how the individual makes sense of all the opportunities, practices and stimuli in a multimodal world. This chapter looks at changing contexts which make up this ecology of learning. As with all ecologies, these factors and contexts are connected in complex ways.

Technological developments and changing views of knowledge and learners

The relationship between the social world, developing technologies and learning cultures has been the topic of wide-ranging educational debate for 20 years, and the degree of change brought about has been deeply contested:

> Whilst there is general agreement that new technologies have brought fundamental changes in communicating to learn within a context of local and global societal change, such changes have been conceptualised from different theoretical perspectives, which can be broadly characterised as "revolutionary" or "evolutionary". These are located in differing historical perspectives on the degree and types of change which are brought about by learning with technologies. (Daly and Pachler, 2010: 218)

Earlier stages in this debate focused on reassessments of the nature of knowledge brought about by technology and the altered social relationships between people which affected the construction and sharing of ideas. This was characterized by work such as Harasim's (2000) argument that a "paradigm shift" had been brought about by a "knowledge revolution". In 2003, Andriessen, Bake and Suthers's evolutionary perspective claimed that a new "knowledge age" had replaced the first "information age" in the contemporary history of learning and technologies. Kress (2003) focused on the potential learning revolution contained within the transformed semiotics of multimodal communication. From a variety of perspectives, some argued (Garrison and Anderson, 2003; Harasim, 2000; Lapadat, 2002; Laurillard, 2002) that the results offered the potential for *improvements* in learning, which

Harasim (2000) claimed to be the twin potentials of "the improved quality of learning" and "the improved opportunities to participate".

A main focus for research and innovation which centred on *improved learning* within formal educational settings was the potentials of technology to bring people together to communicate through language, particularly text-based media. Garrison and Anderson have argued that the key potential of e-learning lies in text-based computer-mediated communication (CMC), which has the "capacity to support reflective text-based interaction, independent of the pressures of time and the constraints of distance" (2003: 6). The impact of technologies on learning via text-based media has been the subject of extensive research in the field. This has focused on various approaches to content analysis of online writing as a means of examining the impact of computer-mediated communication on participants' capacities to conceptualize and to "think through writing" (e.g. Strijbos et al., 2006; Xin and Feenberg, 2007; Daly, 2008b).

The emergence of Web 2.0 technologies has brought a further challenge to orthodox ideas about the creation and distribution of knowledge. Through social networking technologies such as blogs and wikis, the web is used differently: "In Web 2.0 everyday users of the web use the web as a platform to generate, re-purpose, and consume shared content. With Web 2.0 data sharing the web also becomes a platform for social software that enables groups of users to socialise, collaborate, and work with each other" (Franklin and van Harmelin, 2007: 4). To participate in "generating", "re-purposing" and "consuming" web-based content, individuals need to develop the capacity to bring cohesion to a vast array of types and formats of digital material. Doyle and Carter (2003) use the terms "weaving" and "sorting" to indicate the type of interactions with material that are required. We find it helpful to think of this in terms of narrative work by which the users "make sense" of content by creating a collection of choices and links by which they navigate and determine what type of relationship they want to have with other users and their content. In a study of blogging, we argue that narrative construction is core to engaging with Web 2.0:

> Narrative construction in order to "make sense" of ... practice across blogs makes considerable demands of the creative and semiotic work to be done by the user, as each blog is a unique configuration of the resources available, organized with varying degrees of attention to "readability" and "accessibility" by the blogger. (Pachler and Daly, 2009: 9)

The process of sense-making is far from limited to engaging with Web 2.0/hypertextual content as an entity in itself. The reader is engaged with a much wider narrative of "being", by which he or she is positioned as an actor in a social context with other social actors and must work out what the experience will be like and how it is conducted. A personal narrative of being is being constructed through the interaction between the user, digital content and other users. Engaging with narrative processes with Web 2.0 confers varying degrees of agency and control of sense-making and participatory practice.

The advent of Web 2.0 technologies is the first technological innovation to seriously challenge the traditional boundaries between "educational" and "real world technologies". They are dissolving, and it becomes harder at institutional level to draw boundaries around "educational" technological innovations and to ignore the impetus from what is going on elsewhere to develop collaborative, learner-centred ways of communicating and learning.

Recently, the shift away from the desktop as the locus of interaction with technology has introduced a new dimension to e-learning. "Sensor technologies" which "allow computational systems to be sensitive to the settings in which they are used" (Dourish, 2004) have moved computing to become embedded in everyday objects. There is a renewed focus on the individual's engagement with technology and the ways in which this development alters personal ways of engaging with the social and material world in exploratory ways.

Haller (2008) argues that now, as these devices bring the concept of "ubiquitous" computing closer to everyday reality, there is a significant shift in the relationship between the person and technology brought about by the latest innovations in display technologies. They bring a degree of intuitiveness which makes working with technology a natural extension of how we "are" in the world and how we "know" it:

> Data are no longer device dependent but follow us across multiple platforms and locations. The impact of Apple's iPhone and an increasing number of videos of multi-touch surfaces available on YouTube,[1] show that users' expectations about using these devices in their daily lives have increased. The reaction to these natural interface implementations has been very dramatic. This is because people are still interested in a simpler way of navigating information and content where the computer interface is not a barrier, but enables them to accomplish tasks more quickly and easily. Multiple metaphors and interaction paradigms using pen, touch, and visual recognition are coming together with

the other elements to create a new experience. In education, intuitive interfaces lower the barriers to using IT, allow for a better understanding of complex content and enhance opportunities for collaboration ... Speech recognition, gesture recognition, haptics, machine vision and even brain control are all improving rapidly to support more natural interactions with these new display technologies. (p. 91)

Haller argues that mobile learning will increase through the availability of electronic paper and bendable displays. The current ways we organize learning in formal education institutions needs to be revised, because mobile learning is much more than "anywhere, anytime" engagement with learning (Pachler, Bachmair and Cook, 2010). Mobile handheld devices such as telephones and personal digital assistants (PDAs) allow learning to take place away from the desktop, but for Kress and Pachler (2007) the significant shift is epistemological. They emphasize that mobile learning is a "habitus"—a way of being in the world—and that "mobility resides in respect to who produces knowledge and how ... those who 'have' it are accustomed to immediate access to the world ... the habitus has made and then left the individual constantly mobile ... a constant expectancy, a state of *contingency*, of *incompletion*, of moving toward completion" (p. 26). These concepts emphasize important aspects of e-learning—understood here as technology-enhanced learning—as embedded within a "whole life" view of the individual and their relationship with wider society.

Socio-cultural practices

UK ESRC reports (2008a, 2008b) provide evidence that a majority of young people live in changed social and cultural conditions brought about by technology, and that this has far-reaching implications for schools and teachers. The message is that educational policy-making struggles to keep up with the realities of most learners' lives, and "the future" is a world which many young people are already experiencing:

While educationalists are rethinking formal learning environments, young people themselves are using new technologies for informal learning in a far wider array of social settings, public and private, shared and individual. (ESRC, 2008b: 4)

Where young people have access to technologies outside of formal education, there is a considerable range of evidence which points out the extent of the divide between young people's experiences of learning inside and outside of school. The *Horizon Reports* (Johnson, Levine and Smith, 2008, 2009; Johnson et al., 2010) and the MacArthur Report (Ito et al., 2008) have shown the extent of immersion in digital cultures of young people in the USA, examining these as new sites of learning. The MacArthur Report is based on a study which explored the impact of digital cultures on the ways classroom practices need to be re-conceptualized, with huge implications for teacher education: "New media forms have altered how youth socialize and learn, and this raises a new set of issues that educators, parents, and policymakers should consider" (p. 2).

For less advantaged sections of society, the pedagogy which exists within educational institutions is crucial to how they gain access to the potentials of these technologies. The Media Literacy Audit (Ofcom, 2008) showed that children in the UK are familiar with the use of key media such as television, games consoles and the internet, by the age of 5, but differences exist in access to technologies according to socio-economic group. There is a "digital divide", and poorer students rely on technology in schools to participate in "media culture"—for example by having broadband access and use of relatively new computers. Clearly, this picture changes all the time, as prices come down, but there is a continuing argument that policy-making for schools and higher education should be rooted in achieving social justice in this area. Policy is needed to "take responsibility to distribute access to these resources fairly, and to compensate thereby for their unequal distribution in society" (Daly, Pachler and Pelletier, 2009a: 17).

The changed nature of personal and home use of technology therefore has implications for practice across education phases. The divide between young people's experiences and expectations of technology and practice within education institutions is a persistent challenge. On transition to further education (FE) and university, there is an expectation that e-learning will be embedded in the learning experience, despite widely varying previous educational experiences (JISC, 2007: 32). Learners expect to use technologies in personalized ways, to enable them to control aspects of their learning environment. For many school-leavers, e-learning involves the appropriation of technologies such as laptops, mobile phones and social software into their lifestyles. Outcomes from research for the Learner Experiences of e-Learning theme of the JISC e-Learning Programme indicate that by the time learners enter post-compulsory education, they have expectations about the role of technologies in their learning. They have already learned to integrate technology with their lifestyles, often in ways which are "unauthorized" by their experiences of compulsory education. They expect to initiate independent searches for information and participate in social networking and mobile ways of accessing and sharing the content of their own lives (e.g. by photo-sharing) as well as the "curriculum". Choices are made about which technologies to use and how to blend them.

The transition between compulsory schooling and FE and HE sectors is a key point where students have disjointed learning experiences, with generally enhanced access to technological infrastructure to support learning, though not necessarily to enhanced pedagogical expertise in utilizing the resources which are available. A report on technologies in the further education, adult and work-based learning sectors (Becta, 2010) lays the responsibility for improvement with "informed and focused leadership" within the sector's institutions, to achieve greater attention to transition experiences for students:

> Access in FE colleges seems to vary according to subject studied, but on the whole the experience is generally one of improvement for the learner in terms of access to online information and resources, given that the use of learning platforms is relatively mature in FE. Work based learning is a mixed bag, but in general also offers increased opportunities for online learning. Overall there is an increasing need to reflect on and address learners' experience of technology in the context of transition between stages and sectors. (p. 6)

Policy-making

Governments around the world have recognized the need to plan strategically to maximize the social and economic benefits of technologies within a context of global competitiveness and constant change—described as the "digital dividend" in *Digital Britain* (BIS and DCMS, 2009). In the UK, "developing the nation's digital skills at all levels" (p. 9) is one of the key objectives viewed as necessary to underpin continuous expansion of capacity and influence within international communications and economic activity. This recent government report issues a warning that we are at the "tipping point" where lack of access to the Internet is an "active disadvantage" to learning and participation in social and economic life. A focus on policy-making aimed at ensuring access to an inclusive information and communications infrastructure is viewed as an essential responsibility of government.

The European Commission's recent 5-year i2010[2] strategy and consultation for a "post-i2010" strategy reflect the ongoing goals of governments to harness the potentials of technology to support education and economic well-being in member states. i2010 is the EU policy framework which aims to promote the contribution of technologies to the economy, society and personal quality of life. The European Report on the Education and Training 2010 Work Programme (European Commission, 2008) found that the impact of technologies on education and training has not yet been as great as had been expected, "despite wide political and social endorsement". The transformation of business and public services through technologies has not yet reached teaching and learning processes. It found that although technologies have the potential to develop a "learning continuum" that would support lifelong learning and embrace formal, informal and workplace learning, this has not yet been realized. *Implementation* of e-learning practices remains a major challenge and the need for "teacher-led innovation" in higher education is apparent (Laurillard and Masterman, 2010).

The report on 27 EU countries' use of information and communication technology (ICT) in schools (Empirica, 2006) found that the *use* of ICT is the third biggest area of shortfall in ICT across European countries, surpassed only by the need to improve pupil access to computers and internet connection. The UK is reported as having among the highest levels of pupil access to computers and availability of digital resources for teachers. These apparent advantages, however, are not matched by enhanced teachers' knowledge and understanding which can utilize them for innovative practice (Becta, 2007, 2008; Daly, Pachler and Pelletier, 2009a, 2009b) and motivation to use technologies creatively and to support collaborative approaches is problematic among UK teachers (Empirica, 2006). Becta (2008) reported a "significant deficit in practice" in schools in England and the persistence of "slow development of learning and teaching using technology".

Higher education in the UK has been the focus of e-learning policy initiatives in two stages over the past decade. The first (2005) HEFCE e-learning Strategy focused on supporting institutions to develop e-learning as part of its overall focus on the "primacy of improving the student learning experience" (HEFCE and JISC, 2005). It was a response to the finding that institutions were still struggling to "normalize" e-learning as part of higher education practices for students and tutors. The concept of "embedding" e-learning began to gain prominence, as it was recognized that the early focus on infrastructure was insufficient to bring about the fundamental pedagogical shifts that were needed to capitalize on advances in technology. It was argued that e-learning contributes to the range of relevant learning experiences for a range of programmes, not just as a substitute for face-to-face contact in distance situations. The Strategy reflected a key challenge:

> E-learning has been criticised for being technology led, with a focus on providing materials, but has relatively recently focused more on the learner and enabling students and other users to develop more independence in learning and to share resources. This change matches the developments in pedagogy and the increasing need to support diversity and flexibility in higher education. (HEFCE and JISC, 2005: 4)

The Strategy was updated in the 2009 Enhancing Learning and Teaching through Technology (ELTT) revision (including a framework for institutions) and the Welsh HEFCW (Higher Education Funding Council for Wales) Enhancement of Learning Strategy. An Enhancement of Learning through Technology (ELT) programme has been introduced to support this initiative, which involves developing enhanced access to a range of resources and subject specialist practice. The revised strategy has focused on the need for individual institutions to embed technologies as part of their overall development of learning and teaching, with a priority to review existing learning cultures and consider the role played by technology in a broad-based shift towards learner-centred and self-directed pedagogic approaches. This is partly in recognition of the fact that institutional practices and pedagogies need to develop as students' expectations and learning contexts change, and that technologies can support this—rather than viewing technology itself as a driver for change. Laurillard emphasizes that university teachers have the responsibility to create the conditions for students to learn, "to create the conditions in which understanding is possible" (2002: 1), and that technologies are fundamental to that, but do not replace the teacher's responsibility. The *Horizon Report* (Johnson et al., 2010) prioritizes the need for higher education institutions to incorporate emerging technologies as part of a revised approach to working with students more broadly, one which takes account of the world which they inhabit:

> It is incumbent upon the academy to adapt teaching and learning practices to meet the needs of today's learners; to emphasize critical inquiry and mental flexibility, and provide students with necessary tools for those tasks; to connect learners to broad social issues through civic engagement; and to encourage them to apply their learning to solve large-scale complex problems. (p. 4)

The report projects that mobile computing and use of open content are the most prevalent new uses of technology which are set to impact on students' access to education and which shape expectations about being able to learn in flexible and user-controlled ways.

The Rose Report (Rose, 2008), which proposed a major revision of policy and curriculum development in English primary schools emphasized that ICT "is fundamental to engagement in society" (p. 15) and should be embedded within the curriculum as one of the "skills for learning and life" as well as being taught discretely. Through all stages of compulsory education and in post-compulsory sectors, the political will and financial investment to embed technologies within the formal educational experience has been present for much of the past decade (the Building Schools for the Future initiative for secondary schools is a further example). Policy-making in the UK has seen a considerable mobilization of funding and resources to support the development of "e-confident" learners and teachers in schools (Becta, 2008; DfES, 2005) who benefit from fully integrated technological infrastructures for learning. Policy-making however has not brought about the anticipated gains that might have been expected.

A pressing contemporary challenge within European states is how to educate teachers in all phases to use technologies to innovate practice. This is in a context where, internationally, increasing numbers of young people inhabit digital cultures to a far greater extent than their teachers. Laurillard and Masterman (2010) identify three core reasons for the lack of teaching development in higher education in the UK as being: the pressure for higher education tutors to conduct research as a primary professional activity; a "cultural bias towards disseminating one's own ideas" which limits engaging with the ideas of colleagues; and lack of time and guidance to support innovation. They conclude that the results of this mean that:

> Although many teachers are using e-learning in some form by now, they are primarily replicating their current practice in a digital environment, rather than exploring ways in which they can use that environment for genuine innovation. That is, much of their

> use of technology is limited to PowerPoint presentations for reinforcing the key points in lectures, online reading materials, and discussion forums in the VLE. (p. xxx)

This is a pattern within formal education contexts. A historical focus on techno-centric aims for practitioner development has been identified as very hard to shift. Centralized training (the New Opportunities Fund), generic skills training, top-down frameworks for training and "one shot" and "one shot plus follow-up" approaches (Jimoyiannis and Komis, 2007) have meant that the potential of technology to enhance the learning experiences of students remains largely unfulfilled (see e.g. reports on Interactive Whiteboard use in the UK: Moss et al., 2007; Preston, 2004). Similarly, there has been relatively little focus on *how* teachers learn with technologies within online collaborative contexts (Dede, 2006; Fisher, Higgins and Loeless, 2006). The importance of secure subject knowledge and subject-based pedagogical understanding has been highlighted for the effective use of technologies in education (Cox et al., 2003), but there is relatively little that examines how professional development with technologies might be achieved. Exceptions to this include proposals for practitioner-centred professional development (see Daly, Pachler and Pelletier 2009b; Laurillard and Masterman, 2010) and action research as a focus for change (Laurillard, 2008a) but there is little evidence of uptake of such approaches, with a main emphasis still on continuous adoption in terms of increasing efficiency and economy rather than pedagogical use.

Policy tensions affecting educational institutions

The concept of "policy tensions" (Hardy, 2008) offers further explanation of why e-learning in terms of innovative pedagogy is hard to embed, even when there is a high degree of technology "uptake" in educational institutions. Cuban's (2001) argument that technologies are "oversold and underused" suggests that practitioners are deeply affected by the way their job is organized and evaluated. "Policy tensions" offers a strong argument for the impact of policy contexts on the development of e-learning in practice.

Hardy's (2008) argument is that policy tensions of two sorts affect practitioner development. These are policy tensions between e-learning and other areas of government requirements and within e-learning initiatives themselves. Hardy has put forward strong evidence that innovation suffers when practitioners experience pressures to work with multiple initiatives which are of a complex nature. The pressure to respond quickly to each reform agenda damages the qualitative achievements of each of them. Such pressures are actually counter-productive of making a sustainable long-term impact. They ultimately "militated against policy support for more context-specific, long-term, inquiry-based, collaborative professional development practices" (p. 103). He suggests that the effects of this are significant within e-learning environments.

Pearson and Naylor's (2006) research indicates that the first type of policy tensions particularly affects learning approaches in the secondary school sector. The high-stakes testing imperative to "perform" against national targets has led to a situation where "teaching in English secondary schools takes place in a risk averse culture, where teaching 'to the test' is a constant temptation and innovations using ICT are difficult to enact" (p. 284). Where professional development is not statutory, and funds for it are not ring-fenced, other policies dominate choices about training priorities. There is a lack of policy linkage between using technologies, enhancing students' learning and gaining higher grades in current testing approaches.

Policy tensions *within* the field of professional development may be a useful way to understand the problem of school leaders feeling the need to "move on" to implement the most current initiative (e.g. home access, learning platforms, electronic assessment), rather than critically reviewing and developing pedagogy. Hardy (2008) argues that these multiple pressures mean that certain forms of professional development "tended to be marginalised" (p. 110). These were the ones that focused on meeting individuals' needs, and which take account of their particular teaching contexts and their individual students. Improving *educational* practices "for their own sake" became secondary to the need to prepare for the latest adoption of technology. To illustrate the argument, a music teacher might use time attending a whole school staff training session on populating a learning platform and not on learning how to design a lesson using podcasts to motivate students' learning in music. There is seldom time to do both. Ultimately, the ideal would be to have podcasting embedded in the learning platform. But the frequent priority is to have a platform, rather than to improve the quality of the learning and teaching which it might accommodate.

A further argument related to this is made by Convery (2009), who claims that practitioners become "victims" of policy-makers' rhetoric about undifferentiated technological benefits for their students. They are encouraged to believe that serial adoption is a moral imperative, rather that reflect critically on what works best to meet the needs of their learners in their specific contexts. The sheer amount of policy-making requiring innovation means that attempts to integrate technologies within rich pedagogical models are inhibited.

In summary, although there has been a marked increase in availability and use of technologies across the education sectors, there is a lack of impact on practice relative to the mobilization of policy-making and resources which has taken place in recent years. The contexts affecting effective professional development are complex and involve multiple stakeholders. Education practitioners would seem to need considerable motivation and support to learn while navigating the contesting pressures and responsibilities they deal with.

Changing personal/public boundaries

Boundaries between the private and the public world dissolve in many ways as a consequence of increased flexibility and user-control over the locus of work-related and private communication. Conole et al. (2008) report a shift in the ways higher education students approach their studies, adopting practices which integrate learning with the rest of their lives. On the basis of the analysis of the data they gathered, they suggest eight features of technological engagement which bring about change in students' learning practices (pp. 521–2):

- pervasive (technologies are used to support all aspects of study)
- personalized (technologies are appropriated to suit personal needs)
- niche/adaptive (particular tools are used for specific purposes)
- organized (technologies are used in a sophisticated manner to find and manage information)
- transferable (skills gained through non-education use of technologies are applied to learning contexts)
- time/space boundaries (changes to where and how students are working)

- working patterns (new working practices attendant to new tools)
- integrated (suiting individual need).

Technology, they argue, is core to the student's practice as a learner, "it is central to how (the students) organise and orientate their learning. The technologies provide them with a rich variety of alternatives for interaction and communication in relation to learning and a flexibility of use which enables them to take control of their learning" (Conole et al., 2008: 522). Educational institutions, their social, cultural and technological structures and inherent practices need to reflect the socio-cultural practices of the everyday lives of students in order not to be perceived as irrelevant by them (see also Pachler, Bachmair and Cook, 2010).

One key affordance of new technologies, for example, is that they allow users to exercise control and determine whether a "space" for communication is private or public. Users do not just generate their own content but also generate the contexts for their learning in and across formal and informal settings (for a detailed discussion see Pachler, Pimmer and Seipold, 2010). "Spaces" for social networking and online participation continually evolve in ways which classrooms have never been able to do, and are certainly controlled in ways which reflect a completely different set of power relations between participants than those found in a conventional classroom. Matt Locke, in a blog post in October 2007,[3] for example, distinguishes six spaces of social media, which represents one way of charting the changing landscape in which learning increasingly takes place:

- secret spaces (SMS, MMS, IM)
- group spaces (facebook, myspace, bebo)
- publishing spaces (Blogger, flickr, YouTube)
- performing spaces (Second Life, World of Warcraft)
- participation spaces (Meetup, twitter)
- watching spaces (mobile, TV).

As Locke acknowledges, there are limitations to this conceptualization, in particular the overlap between some of the categories as well as their existence offline as well as online. And we are far from suggesting that some kind of utopian experience is ensured along with these choices. What it captures however, is the capacity of the users to engage with "context-making", by which the learners are agentive in constructing the conditions for their own interactional experiences: "Context is continually created by 'minds in motion' within distributed learning systems" (Sharples, 2007). By this Sharples accords a high level of agentive capacity to minds which interact to determine the meaning of things and the outcomes for the participants. "Context is a dynamic and historical process constructed through interaction between people, technology, objects and activities within a pervasive medium to enable appropriate action" (Sharples, 2007).

Ultimately, this way of conceptualizing e-learning recognizes that the dynamic social and cultural changes which technology invokes have consequences for "who we are"—not just what we do. Godwin-Jones (2005) discusses the notion of the "third space" which is "created" by the "net generation" of people who fully inhabit the range of contemporary technological practices. These individuals use technologies to bring things (social relationships, ways of communicating and representing) into being which could not have existed before. These things are not easily captured, described or categorized, and they keep evolving, shaped within the ecology of those spaces. Inhabiting the environment of the "third space" is another instance of "habitus" or "being" in the world, where the process of bringing into being is a main experience rather than the achievement of stable ways of communicating and developing ideas.

This user-centred and agentive perspective is still a long way from the experience of most learners in schools and further and higher education settings—including those which are rich in technology. The MacArthur Report (Ito et al., 2008) claims that "notions of expertise and authority have been turned on their heads" (p. 2) and institutions need to capitalize far more on the informal, collaborative, peer-learning networks which their students inhabit. This would constitute a considerable shift in the ways that formal education has been organized to date.

Electronic mobile devices, especially mobile phones with a wide range of functions, are more and more central features of our everyday lives. Yet, they remain mostly excluded from schools and from key aspects of post-16 education. Whilst media use in everyday life and formal education belong to separate socio-cultural practice domains, the devices and services prevalent in everyday life offer considerable potential as learning resources. This we consider to be one of the main challenges in coming years for educational institutions which have been slow, on the whole, to incorporate the divergent social and cultural realities of students' lives into learning practices.

Challenges for schools, post-16 colleges and universities

Like all learning, e-learning needs to start with the very young and become embedded in the everyday practices of schools as learners move through compulsory education and on into the non-compulsory sectors and to work. There is rich potential for e-learning to become embedded in schools in the UK—the technological infrastructure is there in most cases, and creative curriculum possibilities have begun to re-emerge. But, the counter-forces at work within the ecology of the contemporary classroom appear to ensure that there is ongoing tension between policy and implementation, between skills agendas and professional knowledge and understanding and between technology-driven priorities and a learning agenda.

In the post-16 college sector, pedagogical practice with technologies is expanding, with greater numbers of tutors using technology to "support learners in being creative and working together" (Becta, 2008). There is a persistent problem however where "a high percentage of practitioners reported they rarely or never did this". There appears to be a particular challenge in this sector, with the casualization of employment and lack of career development resulting in less advanced teaching expertise involving technology.

This not only relates to school-leavers but also to older learners returning to education: "Achieving fair access to technology for … adult learners is a continuing challenge. Older learners are less likely to have access … those returning to study or training over the age of 45 are likely to have limited skills in using technology."

In higher education, e-learning has been a focus within a recent UK government paper: *Higher Ambitions: The future of universities in a knowledge economy* (DBIS, 2009). A brief but significant section (pp. 78–9) makes three points which set out expectations for change:

- University leaderships will have to take responsibility for driving the use of new technologies throughout institutions.
- Students should leave university with a competent mastery of online modes of communication and information transfer.
- Information about how technologies are used in each course will be available to students as they choose their options.

As with all policy-making, it is in the implementation that we will see how the ecological factors at work are brought to bear on the rate and nature of change. It is perfectly possible for mastery of online communication to avoid engagement in genuinely learner-centred and self-directing practices. Information about how technologies are used does not necessarily equate with innovative pedagogy in practice. To bring about far-reaching implementation of change across the education sectors is a considerable challenge, but questions about e-learning within educational experiences are firmly on government agendas.

Conclusion

In this chapter we have explored the key contexts affecting e-learning, and how technologies are increasingly blurring the boundaries between formal and informal learning opportunities. Currently, most formal provision and practitioner development lags behind the digital experiences and expectations of new generations of learners about how to engage with the world. There are certainly ample examples where e-learning has become embedded in pedagogical approaches, but these are not a main experience and the relationship between socio-cultural, economic life and formal educational experiences is potentially open to increasing schism rather than convergence. An ecological perspective helps to consider the ways in which a variety of contextual factors co-exist in complex ways and affect the chances of successful change, despite political intention and the deployment of resources and availability of technologies within education.

Notes

1 http://www.youtube.com/results?search_query=multi+touch.
2 http://ec.europa.eu/information_society/eeurope/i2010/key_documents/index_en.htm.
3 http://test.org.uk/2007/08/10/six-spaces-of-social-media/.

Theories, Concepts and Models 3

Chapter Outline

Introduction   57
The shared construction of knowledge   61
Laurillard's Conversational Framework   63
Computer-mediated communication   64
CMC as a literate learning practice   65
Participation   67
The individual and agentive dimensions of e-learning   71
Theoretical perspectives on practitioner development   75
Conclusion   78

Introduction

The factors which contribute to the complex, evolving nature of e-learning have been explored in the first chapters of this book. This chapter explores the ways in which e-learning has been conceptualized in relation to this. Theoretical perspectives on e-learning are located in a range of disciplines, including learning theory, media education, informatics and socio-cultural theory. Approaches are also interdisciplinary, with a variety of fields each contributing to how e-learning can be understood in the context of wider perspectives on learning practices.

Garrison and Anderson's (2003: 2) argument that the transition from individual, primarily content-based learning practices, to collaborative, knowledge-making ones, is an "uncertain process", helps to explain why there inevitably exists a wide range of theoretical perspectives on the impact on learning of evolving technologies. They argue that we are currently in a "gradual development phase" in which participants are part of a very recent, and constantly accelerating history of change in how learning can be organized and conceptualized. The shift away from the transmission-focused "information age" (Andriessen, Baker and Suthers, 2003) denotes an altered perception of people as having the capacity for agency, who share responsibility for making their knowledge through collaborative processes. This, however, offers a fundamental challenge to transmission and content-focused models for learning which persist still in many post-compulsory formal education settings.

This book is not concerned with informatics or scientific disciplines, but it is worth mentioning here that the scope of theoretical perspectives on e-learning is extensive and includes work which conceptualizes e-learning as new ways of processing and transforming "information" as well as participating in social and cultural practices. Informatics explores the relationship between natural and artificial systems in order to understand how information is transformed. Such an emerging discipline signifies the shifts within science as well as the social sciences which have taken place in order to understand the representation and processing of information within such systems. For example informatics encompasses cognition, computation and communication and brings together aspects of existing disciplines such as computer science and artificial intelligence with cognitive science and thus draws on disciplines such as mathematics, biology and psychology. E-learning has been described as a "chameleon field" (Snyder, 1998: xxv), such is the rate of development of ideas which alter the ways we can think about and research this social, cognitive and technological phenomenon. It is important, therefore, to recognize the extent of the far-reaching, interdisciplinary developments which have taken place across a broad spectrum of "subjects" beyond the social sciences.

Our focus here, though, is on ideas about learning with technologies as a social phenomenon, as cognitive and related to engagement in social and economic life. As examined in Chapter 1, there are overlaps between these strands. Like all "learning", e-learning is a complex of strands which each frame the ways it is possible to talk and think about it. We do not claim to offer a complete map of the "e-learning" conceptual territory. Any such "map" will be out of date almost instantly. Eclecticism and adaptation within the field has enabled innovative and interdisciplinary ways of thinking which relate to the rates of technological and socio-economic change which impact on learning with technologies. But the sheer range of perspectives presents a challenge in deciding how to navigate the very differing theoretical approaches which exist.

Various ways of organizing thinking about theoretical perspectives on e-learning have been developed. Conole et al. (2004) distinguished three types of learning theories, according to their pedagogical focus: those related to individual or social forms of learning, their degree of concern with reflection and in relation to information or to experience. Mayes and de Freitas (2004, 2007) have classified theories into three perspectives, *associative*, *cognitive* and *situative*, which contain several areas of overlap but which link broadly to differing pedagogical models.

Haythorntwaite et al. (2007) locate six theoretical perspectives within a view of e-learning as an "activity system", constituted by "its technologies, people, institutions, purposes and embedding contexts, in a complex assemblage, resting on the interactions of multiple factors in multiple contexts". They argue that contemporary theorizing about e-learning needs to address the implementation or enactment of learning design. The core need, they assert, is for new theories and models of learning "addressing learning in its ICT context", which take account of three core foundations for contemporary theory-building: "formal and informal learning; individual and community learning; and new practices arising from technology use in the service of learning". The researchers offer six theoretical perspectives which are located in these elements, which address learning in relation to context:

- living technologies (Bruce), by which technologies can be understood as part of an ecological system and are intrinsically linked to the realization of innovative practices;
- co–evolution of technology and learning practices (Andrews), by which technologies and learning are seen as mutually evolving and interconnected, resisting "causal" analyses of e-learning;
- technology and social tie formation (Haythornthwaite), which draws on social network theory to examine how technology contributes to the formation of differing ties between learners in relation to varying types of media contexts;
- community-embedded learning (Kazmer), which examines the ways in which online learning experience permeates and affects the wider social context, including the workplace, and vice versa;
- learner-leaders (Montague), by which students are active participants in a learning community, both learning and leading by sharing information, experiences, and opinions with their peers; and

- braided learning (Preston), by which a community of online learners engage in textual exchange and formulation of ideas, leading to the generation of artefacts to be shared outside the community and ultimately affecting policy and action.

All these authors indicate that "categories" or "theories" are contingent, or what Haythornthwaite et al. (2007) call "emergent", and are, therefore, consistent with an ecological view of e-learning. Our approach in this chapter is not to propose a "taxonomy" of theoretical types or positions. Our aim as educational researchers is to prioritize perspectives which foreground educational purposes to do with enhancing the capacity for individuals to engage in social and cultural exchange and increase inclusion in social and economic life. This introduces an ethical dimension to our focus.

Early technocentric preoccupations within the field are not part of the discussion in this chapter. While thinking was, understandably, focused on the "how" of learning with technologies, considerations about the purposes of education were given less prominence. Oliver (2003) sums up the chief challenge for conceptualizing e-learning, arguing that it is only when it is properly "embedded" that we will be able to focus on the things that really matter in education—the learning of individuals, and technology's "educational, social or moral impact" (p. 159).

> We must recognise that all learning involves technology, it is simply a matter of how familiar we are with it … [we should] find ways of making taken-for-granted technologies visible, so that we can re-interpret these practices not as simple skills … but as forms of cultural literacy. (Oliver, 2003: 158)

In this chapter we focus on the "learning" dimensions of e-learning to examine theories which are concerned with the positive transformational force of practices involving technologies which contribute to what might be termed "cultural literacy": they contribute towards desirable educational, cultural and social goals. We adopt a "sociogenic" (Koschman, 2003) view of e-learning. Koschmann's concept is based on a view of learning as the appropriation of available resources, social and technical, by which an individual is able to think about and make sense of the world. This view extends to considering the most developed forms of interdependent learning, which are rooted in the collective resources available within a community of learners, all of whom do not have to make contact with each other directly in order to participate in the changed understandings, both individual and social, which emerge.

As such, learning is conceived of as a *practice* involving technologies in connection with people and existing knowledge, which is subject to both internal and social processes aided by technologies which render it meaningful. Such a view resists ways of explaining learning as an individual practice involving conscious acquisition-focused efforts to appropriate external, pre-existing knowledge.

A variety of concepts and related pedagogical models have developed from this premise, based on theory which is concerned with the nature of individual and social roles and actions of e-learners and the achievement of ethical goals in education. We explore theoretical views on aspects of *practice* by which individuals connect with, and contribute to, the development of knowledge as a shared cultural artefact. They all, in their different ways, provide insights into the complex relationship between elements in the learning process, human and technological.

The interrelationship between the private and the public, the individual and the social is at the heart of this perspective on e-learning, and has informed learning theory focused on the shared construction of knowledge, communication and participation, which are our present focus.

The shared construction of knowledge

A central theoretical concern is the relationship between individual meanings and the shared social contexts within which knowledge is developed. There are varying views on the degree to which "knowledge" in (e-)learning contexts can ever be a matter of individual cognition. Garrison and Anderson (2003) argue that, while community is an essential constituent of learning, it is the individual that is the locus of knowledge creation within e-learning: "While knowledge is a social artefact, in an educational context, it is the individual learner who must grasp its meaning or offer an improved understanding" (pp. 12–13). There are differing theoretical priorities in relation to the degree of individual or shared/collaborative cognitive development. Koschmann (2003) asserts that there needs to be a theory of e-learning that explains cognition as rooted in various forms of social relations, which he terms: "social conflict", by which constructive interaction is generated by dialogue that promotes conflict; "social practice", where learning is seen to involve "transformations in community membership and social identity"; and "distributed cognition", where there is a shift "from arguing to learn to learning to argue", that is, from viewing learning as a process of acquisition to one of participation. Learning is thus conceptualized as *a way of engaging*. His "social conflict" view posits that: "learning … occurs through a process of conceptual adaptation or accommodation in response to an intrusion or disruption" (Koschmann, 2003: 263).

Some constructivist theories of learning within new technologies have emphasized "epistemic conflict" or the clash of differing opinions and ideas as a core element (Harasim, 2000; Koschmann, 2003). In this "social conflict" view, interaction based on conflict is posited as having a causal effect on cognition, although the link between the conflict model of social relations and cognitive transformation is not clear, but implies an accommodation or adaptation by the individual brought about by the social relations of conflict.

Whatever the balance between individual and social construction of knowledge, all such positions derive from a view that what is "known" is that which carries a shared orientation towards its meaning, arrived at through collaborative processes which are conducted through language. The Vygotskian origins of theories of concept formation centre on the "significative use" of language, which is prompted "not from within but from without, by the social milieu" (1986: 108). Warschauer's (1999) notion of computer-mediated communication (CMC) as "a potential intellectual amplifier" focuses on the "intersection" between interaction and reflection as being "of critical importance in cognition" (p. 5). This intersection has been the focus of considerable examination to understand the relationship between thought and language interaction in e-learning environments. Mercer's (1995) work on spoken language interaction in social contexts offers a "sketch" of the nature of learning through language interaction in social constructivist contexts. "This is a social, historical process … so that the knowledge that is created carries with it echoes of the conversations in which it was generated" (p. 84). It reminds us that e-learning sits within broader socio-cultural analyses of learning.

Social constructivist theories have taken as a premise that coming to "know" something is not an act of individual cognition alone, but is a process of engaging in the social world and mediating the sense that is made of it through some form of sign which is communicable to others and around which shared meanings can be forged. Discourse is a major catalyst in the interplay between the individual and the social, the private world and the public as a means of constructing knowledge.

Other emphases have also derived from Vygotsky's work. Luckin (2006, 2007) proposes a framework derived from Vygotsky's Zone of Proximal Development (ZPD), his theory by which a person becomes actively involved in dialogue which supports another's learning activity, so that the learner has an active role in constructing meaning and is able to progress further than they could have done alone. Luckin's "Ecology of Resources" (2006, 2007) invokes a wide range of social, cultural and technological resources which constitute the context within which a learner progresses. She developed the concept of the ZPD as a form of "context" in which "productive interactivity" takes place. Within her framework, an e-learner engages with a "Learner Ecology of Resources", which supports a process of mediations conducted via "Organizing Activities" including teacher and learner interaction with technologies as well as with each other.

Laurillard's Conversational Framework

Laurillard's Conversational Framework (2002, 2007; see also Chapter 1) has been a highly influential frame of reference for conceptualizing interaction between individuals in learning contexts, underpinning knowledge construction. The Conversational Framework captures cycles of interaction between learners and teachers involved in concept formation. It is predicated on an iterative process of back-and-forth exchange between learners and tutors, skilfully managed by the tutor/moderator as expert. Laurillard emphasizes the need for iterative dialogue between teacher and learner, because it is the teacher who takes responsibility for "elicit[ing] from the student a new way of experiencing a concept, which is constituted in the person–world relationship" (2002: 77). This calls for a judicious degree of tutor intervention, which must try not to repress or over-influence student contribution—a difficult thing to achieve, and premised on notions of academic discourses which are acceptable in the formulation of knowledge. It is based on a stratified conception of knowledge, in which players do not have equal parts in constructivist processes. Laurillard (2002) acknowledges the "pedagogical advantage" of "student control" in e-learning contexts, but argues that there are no studies to suggest that "this is the kind of medium where students can be left to work independently" (p. 151). Her reservations regarding student–student interaction as a prime learning process relate to a position that there are different "orders" of knowledge about the world, and that "second order knowledge" (or academic knowledge which is "fixed") is the domain of tutors whose job it is to ensure it is made available to students: "if you accept that academic knowledge is knowledge of descriptions of the world and will become known through operations on descriptions, then teaching must be a dialogic process" (p. 71). Laurillard's context for this argument is chiefly undergraduate education, and reflects a perspective on HE contexts where "experts" are necessary to intervene in student learning. Laurillard distinguishes the needs of undergraduates from postgraduates, claiming that mostly it is only at postgraduate level that university courses can aspire to conditions which enable students to learn independently as a "community of scholars" (p. 2), being self-directed.

It may be significant however, that the majority of her examples are taken from positivist disciplines, such as mathematics and science, and refer less to the contribution made to "knowing" by the learner in humanistic subjects in which meanings are not fixed but are more open to interpretation and dispute.

Computer-mediated communication

Such iterative and dialogic perspectives have underpinned the prevalent form of e-learning within formal post-compulsory educational contexts since the 1990s—CMC. Although more diversity is developing with the appropriation of digital video technology and mobile devices in these sectors, text-based asynchronous exchange is still a main e-learning approach. As a constructivist practice it has been described by Harasim (2000: 53) thus:

> The student presents, defends, develops, and refines ideas. To articulate their ideas, students must organise their thoughts and information into knowledge structures. Active learner participation leads to multiple perspectives on issues, a divergence of ideas, and positions that students must sort through to find meaning and convergence. Cognitive growth and development of problem-solving skills depend on epistemic conflict, that is, the collision of adverse opinion ... Students encounter opportunities to experience and resolve academic controversies in the online discourse environment.

Despite theoretical underpinnings, it has been acknowledged that, considering the proliferation of CMC in HE, "what is surprising, and cause for concern, is that we know so little about the use of this medium to facilitate learning" (Garrison and Anderson, 2003: xi). Laurillard (2002) argues that greater scrutiny is needed of whether CMC can "succeed in enabling learning" through collaborative practices:

> It remains a strong belief, given new impetus from the significance of "communities of practice" (Wenger, 1998) ... but ... the properties of a medium do not determine the quality of learning that takes place. (p. 148)

Rourke and Kanuka (2007, 2009) and Veerman, Andriessen and Kanselaar (2000) have pointed out that despite considerable investigation since the 1990s into online discussion in HE, there is little empirical evidence that engaging with online discussion leads to any significant increase in critical thinking for participants. The same issue is emphasized with reference to the professional learning of adults in CMC by Fayard and DeSanctis (2005): "little is known about the evolutionary dynamics of conversations and how these interweave to produce an ongoing, self-sustaining professional development forum". Rovai's (2002) survey of the learning effectiveness of CMC concluded that it is the pedagogical design of the course that matters more than the practice itself, that is, there is no intrinsic impact on learning of CMC. It is not sufficient to focus on the technological aspects of CMC as liberating participants from the conventional constraints of time, space and physical context which provides altered conditions for the learning transaction. In the text-based asynchronous environment of CMC, a major theoretical focus to address this challenge has been on e-learning as a literate behaviour. Literate behaviours for learning centre around participation in textual "thinking" through: augmentation, peer learning, adaptation and modification of expressed ideas.

Computer-mediated communication as a literate learning practice

Theoretical perspectives on text-based CMC have at their core the fact that it is a practice based on exchanging language. CMC as an interactive literate practice allows the adaptation of interaction-based theories of language and knowledge construction which have their roots in Vygotsky's (1986) work. This is about *evolution* in learning practices within a conceptual continuum based on the properties of language to enable the construction of thought, within spoken, written and email exchange. The asynchronous time-lapse facility of CMC is the central element here, where Garrison and Anderson (2003) argue that "students have more time to reflect, to be more explicit and to order content and issues" (p. 26). This is captured by Lapadat's (2002) metaphor that interactive writing "bootstraps the construction of meaning":

> An integral element in the conceptual development that takes place in … online courses … is the interactive textual environment … is particularly facilitative of both social and cognitive construction of meaning because the nature of interactive writing itself bootstraps the construction of meaning.

The textual and social interactive aspects of CMC are frequently described as mutually defining and inseparable elements of learning: "Computer conferencing and networking enable communication that is best described as a form of discourse-in-writing" (Harasim, 2000).

Although it is now almost de rigueur to claim that CMC is the natural heir of f2f collaborative learning practices—for example: "At the core of the e-learning context is a collaborative constructive transaction" (Garrison and Anderson, 2003: 4)—the notion of a "continuum" in literate practices is complex. Whilst electronic discourse uses language that is on a continuum between speech and writing, the relationship between electronic writing and the properties of speech and writing is "uncertain" (Snyder, 1998: xxvi). Claims have been made for online asynchronous text-based exchange as a "way of talking" between participants who are "conversationalists" (Lapadat, 2002). The concept of CMC as a "hybrid" practice is important to a conceptualization of participants "talking" or "telling" within a professional learning context. By "hybrid", spoken and written socio-linguistic practices are brought together (Baron, 2000), thus allowing for informal or freer exchange as "conversation" as well as crafted academic discourse, creating a new context for learning which blurs the boundaries of formal and informal uses of language for learning. Via CMC the *multiplexity* or hybridity of online writing allows the properties of written language to appropriate and adapt the properties of talk. On this basis CMC has been argued to incorporate a "spectrum of resources" (Finnegan, 2003) or literate practices which operate in online interaction to affect learning. Lapadat (2002) argues that it is the "conversational" property of talk as interactive and continuous which is adapted by CMC and which facilitates learning. Lapadat's "characteristics" of the asynchronous conference result in "interactivity and continuity that have the "feel" of conversation". The "feel" of the conversation is altered however, by asynchronous exchange.

> Because the asynchronous medium relieves the conversational-ists of the constraints of communicating in real time, there are some interesting consequences for the kinds of thinking, writing and discursive interaction that take place. (Lapadat, 2002)

This is largely, Lapadat argues, because CMC confers participant control over thinking processes, which makes deeper engagement with concepts possible through the effects of writing and reading messages within the space allowed by time-lapse between postings within a structured, topic-focused environment.

Participation

A significant contemporary perspective on e-learning within post-compulsory educational settings is concerned with understanding learning as a participatory practice. This includes a focus on the role of community in supporting learning and contributing to collaborative knowledge construction, and on the influence of technology-supported learning environments where social interaction and conceptual development are twin pedagogical concerns. The concept of participation within a community underpins socio-constructivist practice by which learners interact through the social and the textual. The relationship between individual cognition and social interaction is argued by Garrison and Anderson (2003), drawing on Dewey (1938), to be at the heart of the "educational transaction":

> An educational experience has a dual purpose. The first is to construct meaning (reconstruction of experience) from a personal perspective. The second is to refine and confirm this understanding collaboratively within a community of learners ... the transaction reveals the inseparability of teaching and learning roles. (Garrison and Anderson, 2003: 13)

Garrison and Anderson draw on Dewey (1938), citing his work on the interdependence of the individual and society as central to their development of the concept of a "community of inquiry" as "a community where individual experiences and ideas are recognized and discussed in light of societal knowledge, norms and values" (2003: 4).

The critical point about participation is the connection between the individual and the social, so that learning is seen as meaningful and agentive, provoking intellectual growth within a community context. They argue that, within a community of inquiry, "cognitive independence" and "social interdependence" are simultaneous and inseparable, and together constitute learning (Garrison and Anderson, 2003: 23).

Researchers into e-learning now consider the nature of relationships between individuals to be more indicative of the existence of community than physical proximity (Preece and Maloney-Krichmar, 2005). Kress (2003) argues that electronic communication creates "presence" as something which is temporal, not geographical. Temporality is to do with participants inhabiting a historical, social and political context which affects the construction of meanings.

Rovai (2002: 4), cites the work of Rheingold (1991) and Hill (1996) who suggest that a "sense of community is setting-specific", and should be viewed as "what people do together, rather than where or through what means they do them". They argue that it is necessary to do research in a variety of contexts to establish the possibilities of what might constitute different types of community. The concept of community, therefore, is not to be restricted to a particular form of structure or environment, but rather defines a collection of people with identities and practices who are brought together by social and learning bonds in which technologies play a variety of roles.

Wenger's concept of a community of practice (COP) links the aspects of "community" with "practice" as a collaborative learning enterprise. The COP emphasizes "a way of talking", a communicative function of community which establishes the meaning of what people do, and enables them to take future actions. Within Wenger's conceptualization, learning is premised on constructivist ideas. For community to be relevant as a core element of e-learning, there needs to be a sense of common purpose and satisfaction of needs through active participation (Rovai, 2002). One of Rovai's criteria for a "sense of community" is having common expectations of learning, citing Lave and Wenger's (1991) assertion that within communities of practice, learning is considered "an integral and inseparable aspect of social practice" (p. 31).

Participatory practice enables individuals to engage in interactive "thinking" behaviours based on shared intellectual activity, involving "scaffolding" and argumentation, by which ideas are adapted and modified as part of ongoing community-building. Whilst there are strong arguments for the impact of these constructivist processes on conceptual change in online contexts, there are questions about the kinds of *intellectual* activity which needs to be identified and also the social relations embedded in online content which affect the nature of the educational transaction.

There are multiple theories of how community impacts on learning, which centre on the notion of interaction. Andrews (see Haythornthwaite et al., 2007) argues that "learning is an effect of *the interaction of a number of communities*":

> The very management of information and resources from different sources, and in different formats, plus the re-shaping of them for particular purposes (steering clear of plagiarism and other forms of appropriation) is an art that could be described as active learning in itself. Learning, in this sense, is a matter of attention, composition and re-composition. The learning is embodied and manifested in the process and the product of re-shaping.

He proposes that there are four "sectors" within which learning happens: real world formal education communities, real world informal learning communities, via conventional media for learning and via multimodal communication. Learning happens "at the individual and community level, and in the interaction between those two levels of operation; and in the four sectors of operation". It happens within "zones" ranging from independent thought to distributed learning, and within the communities that support the learning and are constitutive of it, together with the four sectors. Therefore, the very processes and actions of participation constitute learning—it is a transformative process.

"Latent tie theory" (Haythornthwaite in Haythornthwaite et al., 2007; Jones, Ferreday and Hodgson, 2008) explores "ties" or social links between learners in online contexts. Haythornthwaite proposes that e-learners who form strong ties build them by using a range of media beyond that prescribed as a minimum requirement, so that they proactively utilize a range of technological resources. Weak ties are formed between e-learners who use only the minimum technological resource required. She argues however, that where there is a "group-wide medium" for participation, then this *creates latent ties* which may form the foundation for building strong ties. She identifies this process as "network formation" and it is a feature of many other theoretical perspectives on community building and learning.

A way of conceptualizing "learning" within an online community is offered by the concept of "weak ties", which focuses on what may be present where little observable interaction takes place. Jones, Ferreday and Hodgson (2008) root their work on such "weak ties" in network theory:

> Network theory would suggest that the strong notions of community contained in CoPs might ignore the importance of the "strength of weak ties" ... The educational focus on strong links and the emphasis on community may have downplayed the many necessary but weak connections that make networks so powerful. (p. 92)

They suggest the importance of "weak ties" which enable learning within relatively "inactive" online communities, drawing on the Bakhtinian concept of all "utterances" as essentially dialogic:

> As Bakhtin states, "Sooner or later what is heard and actively understood will find its response in the subsequent speech or behaviour of the listener" (Bakhtin, 1986: 69) ... For Bakhtin, even a monological utterance is full of dialogic overtones. As he explains, "In reality, and we repeat this, any utterance, in addition to its own theme, always responds (in the broad sense of the word) in one form or another to others" utterances that precede it" (p. 94). For the purposes of our argument, this idea is important since it relates to our discussion of latent links and suggests that the process of reading a post might be seen as dialogical, or at minimum, to have dialogical overtones. If a member of a forum reads a posting, and this then has an impact on their subsequent activity, they can be seen as having entered into a learning dialogue even if they do not formally respond to the posting. (Jones, Ferreday and Hodgson 2008: 92)

This is significant in terms of understanding Koschmann's (2003) concept of learning as the appropriation of socio-genic resources within a community of learners, which may not require extensive iterative dialogue.

Rovai (2002) identifies eight factors affecting community for online learning:

- transactional distance
- social presence
- social equality
- small group activities
- group facilitation
- teaching style
- learning stage
- community size.

A different focus on "cognitively productive" online social interactions is favoured by McLoughlin and Luca (2000), who identify actions which denote social interactions to support learning: offer, receive, exchange, explain and elaborate, share, give, challenge, monitor, engage, negotiate. These ways of conceptualizing how community affects learning in online interaction favour actions and organizational features, but avoid focusing on the content of the interaction itself. There is a difficulty here, in that there can be tendency to conflate social actions with conceptual change, and attend to outward social actions as indicative of something which is multiple, complex and to do with attitudinal and conceptual shifts which may be very subtle. Without a focus on transformed meanings, it is hard to discern whether "interaction" is related to conceptual shift.

Work on this challenge has been conducted through a series of research projects (Anderson and Kanuka, 2003; Anderson et al., 2001; Garrison and Anderson, 2003; Garrison, Anderson and Archer, 2001) which have made a significant impact on ways of understanding the conceptual work going on within online communities. Their "community of enquiry" model looks at the relationship between the social, cognitive and teaching presence by systematic qualitative content analysis (QCA) of online textual discourse. There has been a continuing discussion (e.g. Daly, 2008b; Strijbos et al., 2006; Valcke and Martens, 2006) of models of content analysis as a research approach, which will be discussed in Chapter 6.

The individual and agentive dimensions of e-learning

So far this chapter has examined the ways in which e-learning has led to a range of ways of thinking about altered relations between individuals and the social context, their roles in knowledge construction and the dissemination and distribution of knowledge. The notion of the individual learner has been subject to review, as ubiquitous terms such as "the networked" society, "social networking" and "distributed learning" would indicate. Early analyses of the individual within e-learning contexts focused on the core concept of "identity" and the impact on the notion of the "self" which technologies bring about. There has been extensive exploration of the potential of e-learning to confer a high degree of individual control over self-presentation and the capacity to assume alternative identities, thus enhancing learning by "escaping" the constraints of the ways gender, age, appearance and ethnicity are perceived within participatory contexts, and relieving pressure on those who might ordinarily be more reticent in conventional face-to-face learning contexts. Blake (2000: 194) commented on the increased power over self-disclosure in relation to online contexts, by which he means the way in which the student can influence, if not control, "the ways in which her tutor 'sees' her as a person beyond a purely academic ego". In Blake's view, this ability to project an "ego" online affects learning so that personal transformation occurs with the learner emerging not only as a "better informed" or "more skilful" person, but also as a "different" person. Increased power over self-disclosure provides a further challenge to the conflation of what is communicated with the learner's actual thinking. It suggests the impossibility of adopting a psychoanalytical approach to understanding online representation as revealing the learner's actual beliefs. Others, however, have suggested that this capacity for "self-representation" is overstated, and that aspects of identity "leak" into learner–learner and learner–tutor relationships (Suler, 2004; Suler and Phillips, 1998). Whatever the degree of self-representation achieved, such representations affect the dynamic of learning relations within e-learning communities.

E-learning has thus prompted exploration of the capacities of learners to control who and how they can "be" by creating coherent narratives of the "self". In particular, there is a focus on the ways in which this prompts deeper engagement with self-reflection and meta-level awareness of the self as a learner. E-portfolios have become a focus of particular interest in relation to this. McAlpine (2005) has suggested that there are significant advantages for portfolio-based learning approaches, based on enabling learners to construct narrative accounts of their learning, enabling a deeper understanding of their learning for both learners and assessors and aiding self-reflection:

The narrative aspect of "e-portfolios as story" has the potential to create self-constructed identities portrayed through the e-portfolio, weaving an individuals' learning and feedback to provide a reflection of who they are and what they have learned. However, this process may require the inclusion of sub-optimal work—such as the first draft of an essay or the reflection that the individual had missed the point of a science lesson. In order for this to be forthcoming, students must be confident in their power to control the narrative.

The use of an e-portfolio for assessment purposes encourages candidates to provide evidence of their achievements and interests. However, in doing so they create a powerful reflection of themselves—a paper trail of their subjective selves, their activities and achievements—in a manner which would not normally be done, except perhaps through private small family collections of photographs and mementos. (p. 384)

There is a warning here that along with the active encouragement or requirement to represent and construct the "self" within e-learning contexts, there is a considerable ethical responsibility on the part of tutors regarding how personal narrative information is collected, surveyed, used and exchanged. Portfolio-based assessment is often understood as a way of encouraging a sense of personal identity as part of the learning process, by narrating a story of personal and intellectual growth over time on the basis of evidence produced by the learning. Learners actively engage with and construct their identities by seeing their learning unfolding (Darling, 2001), developing awareness of their accomplishments and how their learning takes place (Brown, 2002) and supporting the translation of theory into practice through reflection (Hauge, 2006). This gives rise to a debate, however, about the ethics of documenting the development of an online identity for purposes of accountability or assessment (McAlpine, 2005). This issue has sometimes been debated in terms of the privacy of e-portfolio data, although it goes beyond matters of data protection. It also concerns the ethics of creating a digital portrait of learners' intimate, subjective selves for others (tutors, peers, employers) to judge or evaluate.

Web 2.0 technologies encourage users to venture into another person's narrative construct—for example by reading blogs, commenting on the content of social networking sites or on photo-sharing sites such as flickr. Where such technologies are incorporated within learning contexts, learners are required to engage in something which has been uniquely designed to organize another person's experiences and understandings in ways they choose—for example by a blogger foregrounding one of several "egos" at different times (Pachler and Daly, 2009). The relationship between identity, learning and Web 2.0 practices such as blogging is an area in need of further exploration and theorization in order to understand the kinds of demands which are made on learners' identities and the agentive potential of such practices.

"Context-making" is a concept derived from the ethnographic study of communities (Hymes, 1994). It is the means by which participants in a community establish their competence as members of particular communities, and proposes that individuals are *makers* of the context in which the community exists. "Context" is a malleable concept, applied to individuals communicating in either a physical space or online. Jones (2002) suggests that the context in which online interaction takes place is made up of the various "models" that people build up in their minds (and in their interaction) of the situation. They construct knowledge—or "models" and use these models to make predictions about the kinds of behaviours which will show them to be "competent" members of particular communities. "Context" is, therefore, not something communication "exists in", but is

> something that interactants create as they go along ... context is a function of interaction and negotiation, bound up with communicative intentions and purposes and dependent on the ways people enact *social presence* and become aware of and interpret the enactment of *social presence* by others. (Jones, 2002: 4–5)

Such a perspective affords a high degree of agency to individuals, whose interaction can shape what things mean and bring into being new conceptions of the self as an individual in relation to others. Sharples (2007) draws on Cole's (1996) distinction between "that which surrounds us" and "that which weaves us together" in his assertion of the agentive capacities of context-creation within electronic discourse communities: "Context is continually created by "minds in motion" within distributed learning systems". By this he accords a high level of agentive capacity to minds which interact to determine the meaning of things and the outcomes for the participants: "Context is a dynamic and historical process constructed through interaction between people, technology, objects and activities within a pervasive medium to enable appropriate action" (Sharples, 2007)—i.e. learning.

The concept of context-making grants a high degree of agency to participants and refers to both individual and social conceptions held by a learning community of what it is they do and how they learn. Key to the agentive dimension of the context-making process is the adoption of roles in each other's learning, where inter-participant exchange and social presence impacts on individual and collective learning and control over knowledge-making processes.

Theoretical perspectives on practitioner development

As discussed in Chapter 2, it is only relatively recently that there has been much focus on theory-building around developing pedagogical practice in e-learning. Technologies, potentially, force practitioners to ask questions about pedagogy that have not been asked before and generate research and theoretical curiosity about pedagogy. Salmon's (2004: 25–37) "Five Stage Model" addressed the needs of learners who were classed as "activists", "pragmatists", "theorists" or "reflectors" (Salmon's adaptation (pp. 72–3) of Honey and Mumford's (1986) typology of learning styles). Her model suggested that the foundations for learning are established in Stages 1 and 2 of online course design, emphasizing that social bonding is the preliminary to successful learning online. Salmon's model has been influential in practitioner training, and it focuses mostly on developing practical strategies rather than theory-building in relation to the development of practitioner knowledge about e-learning.

"Learning design" is a concept which has interested several thinkers within practitioner learning theory and more widely. For Kress (2000), "design" is about the appropriation and transformation of existing resources by an individual in order to represent what it is they need or desire to communicate. It is essentially bound up with *intention* and *agency* on the part of the individual and denotes the ways in which they harness the multi-modal resources which have been made available by others within social contexts. Such a view of agentive and proactive engagement with existing resources in relation to *intention* is a recurrent focus in theoretical analyses of practitioner learning. Laurillard and Masterman (2010) propose that a form of meta-engagement with their own e-learning is an essential foundation for practitioners to develop pedagogy which is theoretically informed. They argue that a new interpretation is needed of practices such as "course design", and that the practice of designing for learning can reflect e-learning activities themselves, by taking place as a set of developments which are online.

"Learning by design" has also been a focus of work (Koehler and Mishra, 2005; Mishra and Koehler, 2006) on how practitioners develop e-learning practice and knowledge. Within formal education settings, the concept of "technological pedagogical content knowledge" (TPCK) was developed by Mishra and Koehler (2006), derived from Shulman (1986). Shulman proposed the concept of "pedagogical content knowledge" (PCK) by which tutors' subject knowledge is transformed by practice, so that the content area of their knowledge is developed into "pedagogical knowledge"—understanding and "know-how" about how ideas and content are "re-presented" for learning and become meaningful to learners. Mishra and Koehler (2006) developed their framework for teacher knowledge to include information and communications technology (ICT), to become TPCK. The framework (see Figure 3.1) describes their adaptation of Shulman's concept of PCK and argues that university tutors learn to use technologies as a further dimension of this. They propose that professional knowledge of subject content, pedagogy and the role technology is deeply interrelated. Engaging with technologies has a transforming effect on what it is to "know" something, and on how tutors think people learn. Pedagogy changes along with transformations in tutors' knowledge about the "content" aspect of their work. They come to realize that further subject complexities need to be explored for example, and that group work is an effective strategy which can be supported by a particular use of technology for students to record and present shared outcomes. The implication is that tutors learn in a continuous integration of developing subject knowledge, application of technologies and deepening understanding of effective pedagogy. It is a holistic process.

Mishra and Koehler argue that:

> Most scholars working in this area agree that traditional methods of technology training for teachers—mainly workshops and courses—are ill suited to produce the "deep understanding" that can assist teachers in becoming intelligent users of technology for pedagogy ... context neutral approaches are likely to fail because they overemphasize technology skills. (2006: 1031–3)

To develop TPCK on a practical level, they developed the concept of "Learning by Design":

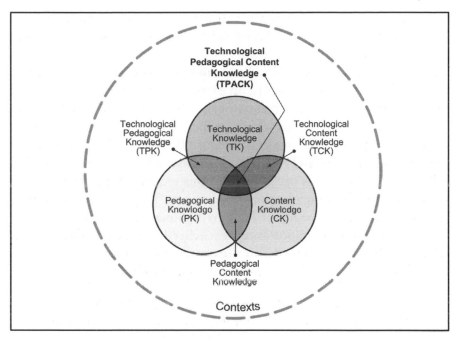

Figure 3.1   Pedagogical technological content knowledge. The three circles, Content, Pedagogy and Technology, overlap to lead to four more kinds of interrelated knowledge
Source: http://tpack.org/tpck/images/tpck/a/a1/Tpack-contexts.jpg

> Whereby teachers learn about educational technology by engaging in authentic design tasks in small collaborative groups. Our approach goes beyond the simple acquisition of skills (something that has been criticized in the teacher education literature). The acquisition of skills approach does not address what we and others believe is a critical issue: that teachers need to develop pedagogical understandings. (Koehler and Mishra, 2005: 97)

This process may involve redesign in the light of critical reflection on trial lessons using ICT. By "design" teachers learn to use technologies in innovative ways, and tailor their use to achieve goals which are specific to their learners. Examples include teachers making digital films, which demand the same skills they might expect their students to use, and redesigning a website as an educational resource in a subject specific area, thus developing judgments about effective learning activities at the same time as developing ICT skills. "Deep understanding" and "intelligent" use of technology for pedagogy involves continuous feedback and review by trying out the methods, and cannot be taught by demonstrations. The teachers need to "live with" the technologies they intend to use with the students.

Angeli and Valanides (2008) have argued, however, that the TPCK framework only presents part of an extremely complex picture of how tutors learn to practise with technologies. They argue that TPCK should acknowledge the particular effects which technologies can have on learning. They refine the model, calling it "ICT–TPCK" and admit that the development of ICT–TPCK "is not an easy task". "Restructuring" of old teaching practices is necessary, and this requires active engagement with risk-taking within a learning community. They thus incorporate a review of original ideas about PCK by Shulman and Shulman (2004) which recognized the importance of teacher learning communities, in which teachers are supported to "learn from experience" and which link individual with shared and institutional reflection:

> Teachers must be trained in powerful learning environments where teaching is situated in real and authentic tasks, and in ways where teachers themselves constitute a part of a larger learning and professional community for the purpose of exchanging perspectives, resolving dilemmas, and confronting uncertainty in transforming classroom practice. (Angeli and Valanides, 2008: 166)

This is why, from an ecological perspective, the ways in which universities operate as learning institutions are critical to developing professional knowledge of how to use technologies effectively.

Conclusion

A "socio-genic" (Koschmann, 2003: 264) view of e-learning includes not only the appropriation of cultural tools and practices for argumentation, but also recognizes their evolution over time. Much of the emergent theory identified in this chapter sees learning very much in line with Koschmann's view, as "a process of restructuring a socially-organized activity". Individuals are involved in "restructuring" processes, involving both restructuring of knowledge and understanding of concepts, and also, essentially, reformulating ideas about what it is to practise as a learner in a collaborative online context. Theory derived from socio-cultural analyses of e-learning as *practice* converge around a view that learning is the process by which individuals appropriate a complex socio-material system rather than a matter of individual cognitive transformation. Koschmann's (2003) theory of "distributed cognition" stresses this is only one among other theoretical views of learning within a community perspective, and that a convergence is needed to overcome views which assign learning as either "social" or "individual". Polarized conceptions of "autonomous" and "collaborative" learning are inadequate to describe the evolution of e-learning. Learners themselves express multiple and contradictory experiences of these (see e.g. Conole et al., 2008; Creanor et al., 2006; Daly et al., 2007). E-learning, therefore, is a combination of individual-cognitive and social-interactionist processes.

Online Learning and Teaching and Learning about Online Teaching 4

Chapter Outline

Learning revisited   81
Affordance   83
Knowledge construction through interaction   83
Supporting collaboration and artefact creation   85
Distributed cognition?   87
A sense of place   90
Pedagogical templates, models and frameworks   91
Conclusion   108

Learning revisited

In Chapter 1, we started to explore the importance of ontological clarity about the notion of learning as a baseline for the planning of effective pedagogical interventions. We noted implicitly, that there is a danger of a weak link between educational practice enhanced by new technologies and learning theory. A study of the literature on technology-enhanced learning shows that the application of new technologies to teaching and learning processes brings the question of what it takes to learn to the fore (see e.g. Ravenscroft, 2001: 149–50). In order to be effective, approaches to e-learning need to try to ensure a close fit between learning theory and the design, implementation and evaluation of interventions.

On this note, we want to start this chapter with some more detailed considerations of learning. From our perspective one fundamental point is the fact that learning is not confined to formal, instructional settings and requires no curriculum or pedagogy (see e.g. Kalantzis and Cope, 2004: 38); instead we understand it as the making of meaning of and through being (including social interaction) in the world. The affordances (we discuss this term below) of new, ultra-portable or mobile technologies, in particular their multi-functionality and convergence with the internet, enhance the potential for, and importance of, learning in informal settings. E-learning arguably shares characteristics of both learning in formal and informal settings. On the one hand it is inextricably bound up in formal educational processes characterized by the conscious nurturing of learning in a community specifically designed for this purpose with its own cultural practices around a more-or-less clearly delineated body of knowledge to which a conscious application of processes (i.e. pedagogy) is applied in order to bring about learning (see Kalantzis and Cope, 2004: 39). At the same time, because mixed-mode engagement takes place away from formal educational institutions, e-learning is also embedded in the learners' everyday life and life-worlds. In our view this fact requires specific design considerations as the form and extent of learning can be understood to be determined by the conditions in which it occurs.

Kalantzis and Cope (2004: 40) posit two conditions, which they consider to impact on learning:

> First, whether a person's identity, subjectivity or sense of them-selves has been engaged; and second, whether the engagement is such that it can broaden their horizons of knowledge and capability.

The first condition, which they call "belonging" they see founded in three things: "the learning ways, the learning content and the learning community" (p. 40). This, incidentally, is also a theme that surfaced prominently in the engagement of philosophers with e-learning (see e.g. Blake, 2000; Kolb, 2000).

The issue of subjectivity is important because it encompasses the concept of learner difference and particularity. How to make learning "gel" for all students (Kalantzis and Cope, 2004: 45) is not at all straightforward, particularly in a context where a tutor—if one exists—may know very little about the learners and in which the learners may comprise a much more heterogeneous group than in traditional face-to-face (f2f) settings, for example by virtue of being dispersed around the world, have different mother tongues and sets of prior educational and/or professional experiences and so on. Learning has to engage with learners' identities (Kalantzis and Cope, 2004: 45), which must be recognized as different from each other, and it must take them into unfamiliar "places", with the places being unfamiliar to just the right degree, that is, with there being just the right distance between the learners' life-worlds and the learning. This represents the second condition, which they call "transformation". The pedagogical challenge according to Kalantzis and Cope (2004), borne out by our work in developing e-learning interventions (see Chapter 1), is to design learning in a way that takes account of these conditions.

Affordance

Commentators on "affordance" (e.g. Derry, 2007; Jones and Dirckinck-Holmfield, 2009; Oliver, 2005) stress the importance of not viewing technology as offering educational advantages independently of the individuals engaging with them and the purposes of that engagement. They stress instead the need to be aware of the particular epistemology, that is, beliefs about knowledge, underpinning the use of technology for learning (see Derry, 2007; Oliver, 2005). Also, affordance is proposed as a relational property, that is, as one that exists in relationships between artefacts and active agents (Jones and Dirckinck-Holmfield, 2009: 17). From this Jones and Dirckinck-Holmfeld (p. 18) conclude that educators might be able to assist learners by suggesting how they might "read" affordance.

Knowledge construction through interaction

One crucial aspect of effective design of e-learning interventions is the quality of communication between the learners and the tutor. As Blake (2000: 184–5) notes, student–tutor interaction in e-learning (and distance learning more broadly) is often characterized by the replacement of a "live" teacher by a "teaching text". Blake notes that this is not to say that the text actually does some teaching, but that the learner actively has to study the text behind which there is a writer who can be described as "teaching at a distance". In models of e-learning based on social-constructivist notions of learning and of knowledge building the "teaching text" is often no longer produced or selected by the tutor (alone) but (co-)constructed by learners. This has clear implications for questions of epistemology, that is, the knowledge base to be taught, and on coherence, representativeness, comprehensiveness, bias and so on. Blake argues (p. 189) that typical academic speech acts—by which he means those whose illocutionary force can be made evident by the use of conventional verbal formulae or from textual or discourse context alone rather than some explicit social setting with concomitant conventions—are well suited to the exclusively textual context of online communication. He sees academic discourse as having its own "linguistic pragmatics" (p. 190). Blake's observation raises an interesting issue, as electronic communication (in asynchronous form such as e-mail or in synchronous form such as real-time chat) tends to be characterized by a degree of informality that sits ill-at-ease with the (perceived) characteristics of academic writing. In our work on the MTeach, a mixed-mode professional online course at Masters level (see also Chapter 1), many students have found it difficult to conceptualize what writing in electronic media as part of a Masters course might and should look like. We identified "genre conflict" existing where participants express "perceived incompatibility between formal and informal modes of language use: 'Do we have to do it academically? Or do we have to do it in a chat form as you would an e-mail?' " (Daly et al., 2007: 455). Blake also notes (2000: 191) that what he calls the "distantiation" inherent in online communication may foster and encourage a more vivid disclosure of learners' "academic identity". In terms of making judgments about learning in online contexts, Blake (p. 193) argues the need for insightful interpretation of learners' written online contributions: "The question is not 'What do these words mean?' but 'What does this student mean [by these words]?'" Finally, for our purposes here and with reference back to our earlier discussion of Kalantzis and Cope (2004), Blake argues (2000: 194) that the online environment affords, and to some extent requires, a degree of intentional self-disclosure about their academic transformation which provides evidence of how learners have become different persons in the process of engaging with the online pedagogical intervention.

A rather different take is proposed by Slevin (2008). With reference to Beck, Giddens and Lash (1994), he sees the importance of a focus on dialogue motivated in the socially produced risk characteristic of late modernity. Based on Giddens (1994) it is argued that a generative approach to risk involves inter alia the need to facilitate and encourage intelligent relationships between organizations, groups and individuals through dialogue rather than authority. This is seen as a preparation for the fact that "decisions have to be taken on the basis of more or less continuous reflection on the conditions of one's actions" (Giddens, 1994: 86), which dialogue arguably supports.

Supporting collaboration and artefact creation

An important role of digital technologies lies in supporting collaboration and artefact creation. Participation in online communities tends to take the form of computer-mediated textual thinking through augmentation, adaptation and modification of expressed ideas (see Daly and Pachler, 2007: 81). Stahl points out (2006: 221) that technology-supported practices of meaning-making are public, observable and socially shared processes. These processes can be seen to enable new ways of thinking as well as often to require a questioning and re-evaluation of personally held beliefs on the basis of the contributions of others, that is, they create so-called "epistemic conflict". One effective way of structuring discussion in online communities is through narrative, understood as a way of understanding, organizing and communicating experience as "stories" (Daly and Pachler, 2007: 56–7), according to Bruner (1985) a "primary form" by which human experience is made meaningful.

> Discourse activities—such as questioning, proposing, arguing, critiquing, negotiating, accusing, repairing, agreeing—are as important as the artifacts around which, through which and into which the discourse moves. (Stahl, 2006: 225)

In short, online participation, "the discourse among individuals, the social relationships that bind them, the physical artifacts that they use and produce" (Jonassen and Land, 2000), can be viewed as central to online learning (see also Hrastinski, 2009). Yet, according to Hrastinski (2008: 1756), the perception of what online participation should look like varies considerably: it ranges from accessing e-learning environments to taking part and joining in a dialogue. Questions arise, for example, about the role of reading or "lurking", as opposed to writing or physical presence, in relation to participation. Given the cognitive activity it requires, can reading online contributions from fellow learners really be classed as a "passive" activity? On the basis of a literature review, Hrastinski offers the following definition of online participation (p. 1761):

> Online learner participation is a process of learning by taking part and maintaining relations with others. It is a complex process comprising doing, communicating, thinking, feeling and belonging which occurs both online and offline.

Such a definition of online participation has clear implications not just for research but, maybe more importantly, for the assessment of online learning: how, for example, can offline thinking best be captured and validated? Stahl (2006: 280) asserts that collaborative accomplishments need to be assessed at the level of the individual, the small group and the community. He also argues (p. 293) that we need to better understand how knowledge and meaning are encapsulated in artefacts, how (groups of) people come to understand these embedded meanings and interpret them. For Stahl (p. 318) meaning-making is essentially a social activity rather than one carried out by individuals who are co-located, and artefacts are embodiments of meaning. This, once again, has profound implications for assessment of artefacts, be they in physical, symbolic, digital, linguistic or cultural form (p. 4). And it raises philosophical as well as practical questions around how the contribution of the individual to an artefact can be judged if its meaning is socially grounded and distributed. Stahl recommends discourse analysis / ethnomethodology as a key method of analysis.

> While meaning inheres in the discourse, the individual group members must construct their own interpretation of that meaning in an on-going way. Clearly, there are intimate relationships between the meanings and their interpretations, including the interpretation by one member of the interpretations of other members. But it is also true that language can convey meanings that transcend the understandings of the speakers and hearers. It may be precisely through divergences among different interpretations or among various connotations of meaning that collaboration gains much of its creative power. (p. 345)

Brown and Adler (2008: 18) highlight another dimension of participation, which they, rightly in our view, consider to be important for success in higher education: participation in small groups. This perspective, according to the authors, shifts the attention from content and its transmission to activities and human interaction around which the content is situated. Consequently, learning is not just "learning about" but also "learning to be" a participant in a subject domain which involves acquiring the practices and the norms of established practitioners in a field or acculturation into a community of practice (p.19).

Gee, in a keynote at the 2009 Handheld Learning Conference,[1] stressed the significance of what he calls "affinity groups" in learning in informal settings, which he considers to have the following characteristics:

1. organized around a passion
2. produce don't just consume
3. smart tools
4. not age related
5. newbies and experts together
6. people mentor and get mentored
7. knowledge is distributed
8. knowledge is dispersed
9. learning is proactive but aided
10. everyone is always still a learner.

In order to be able to harness the potential of "affinity groups", the design process of online learning experiences should take cognizance of these characteristics. This list for us holds great relevance for the design of online learning experiences in formal settings.

Distributed cognition?

As already indicated in Chapter 1, we view both the personal and the social perspective as essential for cognition. Theories of knowledge construction are also premised on the notion that coming to know something is not an act of individual cognition alone but instead a process of engaging in the social world and mediating the sense made of it (see Daly and Pachler, 2007: 81). Stahl (2006: 197) reminds us that language is the medium of knowledge and that it is grounded in our life experiences, in our physical embodiment, in our sense of rationality, in cultural traditions, in the interaction patterns of communication and so on. In other words, knowledge is a socially mediated product, never absolute and always subject to questioning, reinterpretation and renegotiation.

The challenge in relation to e-learning, therefore, is not so much a debate about details of theoretical explanations of (distributed) cognition but, instead, to identify what is educationally effective and how educational practice best be designed.

Hewitt and Scardamelia (1998: 81) take a combined situative and cognitive interpretation of distributed cognition and propose a greater distribution of regulatory processes, including those related to curriculum goals and assessment of progress, and consequently see the central challenge in the ability to monitor progress and refine goals, not just distributing tasks and sharing ideas. In their model of a knowledge-building community, the following features are important (pp. 82–4):

- classroom activity defined by advances in knowledge rather than completion of tasks
- greater access to distributed expertise
- student-centred artefacts as mediators of distributed cognition.

Learning can be seen to take place in communities and to be facilitated by artefacts, which in turn sustain the communities that generate them (Stahl, 2006: 220). Unsurprisingly, therefore, communities of practice (COPs) (see e.g. Lave and Wenger, 1991; Wenger, 1998) are often used in the world of e-learning as a conceptual frame for the design of pedagogical interventions, in particular to foster learning through "talking within practice" as well as collaborative meaning-making. According to Wenger (1998: 72–3) COPs are characterized by shared enterprise, mutual engagement and shared repertoire. A central issue for us here is the relationship between individual meanings to the social artefact that is knowledge (see e.g. Garrison and Anderson, 2003: 12–13). Another relates to the specific configuration of the three structural properties of COPs to maximize learning:

> Is it, for example, more productive for (learners) to be organized through a pedagogical model based on relatively weak ties among the participants, or is it more productive to be organized in accordance with a pedagogical model facilitating the development of the strong ties in a community of practice or perhaps a blend of both? (Jones and Dirckinck-Holmfield, 2009: 22)

Online participation is linked to the field of computer-supported collaborative learning (CSCL), which can be seen to be underpinned by a variety of related and overlapping theoretical perspectives such as knowledge communication, knowledge construction, interaction, intersubjective learning or knowledge building (see e.g. Suthers, 2006). In view of our discussion of Kalantzis and Cope (2004) and Blake (2000) above, intersubjective learning, which goes beyond information sharing and includes the sharing of interpretations and the joint creation of interpretations through interaction is particularly fruitful. According to Jones and Dirckinck-Holmfield (2009: 11), CSCL is a complex system characterized by non-linear interrelationships between variables, including thresholds, lags and discontinuities. These characteristics pose challenges for learning. Other issues that may impact on learning according to Jones and Dirckinck-Holmfield (p. 13) are: time shifts, place, digital preservation, public/private boundaries, forms of literacy and content. They conclude—with other commentators—that technology disrupts and disturbs traditional boundaries, and we would add processes, of education. Jones and Dirckinck-Holmfield (p. 15) argue that new technologies must be seen in the context of a relational infrastructure which, Star and Ruhleder (1996: 113) suggest, consists of eight dimensions:

- embeddedness (integrated in social structures and practices)
- transparency (can be used without removing focus from the task)
- reach or scope (goes beyond individual tasks or processes)
- learned as part of membership (an inherent part of an organization)
- linked with conventions of practice (shapes and is shaped by practice)
- embodiment of standards (builds on standards and conventions)
- built on an installed base (must relate to existing technologies)
- visibility upon breakdown (loses transparency and is drawn into focus when it breaks down).

This list of dimensions reminds us vividly of how complex effective use of digital technologies is, and, as they are shaped by practice, infrastructures supporting online and e-learning must be viewed as dynamic and not static.

In the context of CSCL, "a field centrally concerned with meaning and practices of meaning-making in the context of joint activity and the ways in which these practices are mediated through designed artifacts" (Suthers, 2006: 662–3), one important aspect of learning is intersubjective meaning-making where the focus is on the group rather than the individual as learning agent. Therefore, from an intersubjective epistemological perspective information sharing in and of itself is insufficient. Instead, the focus is on jointly created interpretations as well as mutual constitution. "An intersubjective epistemology is distinguished from common ground by assuming a participatory process within which beliefs are enacted … without necessarily being mutually accepted" (Suthers, 2006: 664). Acts of interpretation may take the form of "predications, commentary, restatements, or expressions of attitude … expressed verbally, gesturally or through manipulations of representations" (p. 668). An intersubjective perspective on CSCL raises the question of how interaction between people leads to learning. Other questions include whether cognitive phenomena exist transpersonally (p. 666). Finally, technology is seen by Suthers (2006) to provide the following unique opportunities for intersubjective meaning-making:

- (im)mutable mobiles (reconfigurability, replicability)
- negotiation potentials
- referential resources
- integration of prior conceptions
- trajectories of participation
- adaptiveness
- reflector of subjectivity.

A sense of place

One important consideration in the context of providing an environment conducive to online learning, according to Kolb (2000), is the requirement of a "sense of place" online and the provision of time for thought and evaluation. He applies the philosophical ideas of Heidegger to the social sciences by delineating the following four dimensions: objects, times and moods, values and individual subjects.

> For an online site to be a place, it needs to be more than a static block of data. It needs … objects to interact with that have some independence and thickness of their own; it needs … times and changes so that it is not always the same but varies according to its own rhythms; it needs … ideals and aspirations and calls to what we might become; it needs … a sense that choices are meaningful in finite careers, that time makes demands and is not unlimited in amount. (Kolb, 2000: 124)

One of the important issues for Kolb (p. 125) is the notion of self-critical inhabitation and deconstruction (but not un-building). The importance of a sense of place is also supported by Jones and Dirckinck-Holmfield (2009: 22) who argue that it "is necessary in order to develop a social and emotional context to sustain social interactions and collaboration".

Dwelling with a sense of at-home-ness can be seen to be linked to norms of expectations for appropriate or inappropriate actions which in turn are important for a place to be perceived as our own (Kolb, 2000: 125–7). Kolb furthermore argues the case for what he calls "playing around with the rules" of an online place for learning as well as possibilities for "departing from the script" (p. 127). He sees the creation of an environment with tools for interaction that encourage a "slowed-down contemplative encounter" as the technological challenges (p. 132). In short, one important characteristic of online participation can be seen to be "place-making". Pedagogical designs for e-learning need to take account of that.

The emergence of social media and Web 2.0 tools have reinvigorated the discussion about spaces and places for learning and we already referred to Matt Locke's typology in Chapter 2. Punie (2007) offers the following typology of characteristics of learning spaces enabled by technology:

- learning spaces are connecting social spaces
- learning spaces are personal digital spaces
- learning spaces are trusted spaces
- learning spaces are pleasant and emotional spaces
- learning spaces are learning spaces
- learning spaces are creative/flexible spaces
- learning spaces are certified spaces
- learning spaces are open and reflexive spaces
- learning spaces as knowledge management systems.

Design of online learning environments should take account of the importance of the concept of space and there should be a direct relationship between the intended uses of the environments and activities taking place therein and their spatial features.

Pedagogical templates, models and frameworks

Laurillard and Masterman (2010), rightly in our view, point out that investment in teacher development around the use of new technologies has only accounted for a very small amount of the overall expenditure on technology in education.

They see this, together with a lack of support from institutions in terms of time and pedagogic guidance as the main barriers for innovative practice. As a result, they argue, practice in the main is characterized primarily by the replication of traditional approaches in a digital environment rather than genuine innovation.

In Daly, Pachler and Pelletier (2009a) we diagnose a similar situation in the context of ICT use in maintained school settings. We argue that the literature provides evidence that many effective approaches to ICT CPD are in place, but they remain localized and there are insufficient means for ensuring that all teachers can access high-quality professional development in this area. In addition, we diagnose an overemphasis on skills training at the expense of deep understanding and application of skills to developing learning and teaching. This we see as linked to a perceived need to address a skills "deficit" in teachers, rather than to develop a focus on pedagogy. Furthermore, we consider there to exist a challenge of developing an appropriate "vision" for ICT among school leaders focused on pedagogy and teacher development.

As a possible solution to this issue, Laurillard and Masterman (2010) propose an approach to teacher professional development through an online environment for learning design to facilitate course and "lesson" planning with new technologies. It is interesting to note that whilst Laurillard (2008: 522) emphatically argues for an education-driven rather than a technology-driven approach to the use of digital technologies and despite warning against teaching being driven by what the technology makes possible (p. 526), she proposes technology as a seemingly important part of the solution, particularly in relation to achieving economies of scale. Examples she gives (p. 528) include emulating small group tutorial discussion through virtual communication, provision of feedback and tracking of learner performance to predict the optimal next task.

Laurillard and Masterman (2008) have worked on two tools, the London Pedagogy Planner[2] and Phoebe,[3] which are intended "to support teachers and lecturers in using digital technologies to engage effectively in learning design within their normal teaching". Ostensibly, these tools provide semi-automation for pedagogical planning and intervention based on guided choice, by offering:

1. support for some personal development in how to teach— there are online learning design tools under development, which are explicitly designed to help teachers gradually

bring learning technologies into their work and link to repositories of existing digital resources in their field;

2. the means to build on the work of others to design their approach—online COPs can offer access to existing learning designs, case studies, lessons learned;

3. the means to experiment and reflect on what the results imply for activity management system can offer a simple authoring environment for the lecturer to sequence a set of learning activities, run it for student groups collaborating online, monitor student progress, offer a simple editing environment to improve it in the light of practice; and

4. the means to articulate and disseminate their contribution—creating a learning activity sequence is one form of articulation of what the lecturer thinks it takes to learn a particular topic, or achieve a particular learning outcome, and the online community is the means to disseminate that idea, once proven, their design and their understanding an interactive learning. (Laurillard, 2008: 530–31)

We think there are grounds to support a less "programmed", whilst nevertheless structured, approach to pedagogical interventions to that put forward by Laurillard and Masterman (2010), namely a so-called template-based approach. This is discussed in the literature as a fruitful way of addressing the challenges inherent in the relative lack of proximity of learners to traditional educational settings as well as for teachers to deal with the complexity of the technological options available to them. So-called templates can take various shapes and forms and should be understood at a metaphorical rather than at a mechanistic level. They tend to have in common the aim of providing learners with a frame for structuring and co-ordinating acts of knowledge construction and of encouraging " 'on-the-fly' recording of thoughts and impressions" (Rüschoff and Ritter, 2001: 227–8) whilst engaging in learning activities. Therefore, an important function of template-based learning can be seen to be "to provide a framework for gathering information, stimulating recall of prior knowledge, and for guiding processes of knowledge construction" (p. 228). According to Rüschoff and Ritter (p. 228) they "permit the learner to proactively participate in the process of ... learning". In this way, templates can be seen to respond directly to what Laurillard (2008: 527) considers learning theorists to agree on about learning, namely that it is not something that happens to learners but an activity they do, that is, *inter alia* as involving meta-cognition, problem-orientation, inquiry-orientation, goal-orientation, "reflection" and social communication.

We drew in our own e-learning design on the MTeach on Rüschoff and Ritter (2001). Based around experiential, mediational and conceptual principles we try to engage learners in the construction of shareable texts which relate to their professional pedagogical practice as teachers and encourage the "on-the-fly" recording of thoughts and impressions whilst examining learning materials including theoretical and conceptual literature, policy documents, case studies and so on.

> The taught modules of the course are based around a series of online discussions and the discussion templates are problem-solving in orientation, encouraging course participants to "go meta" about their teaching (see e.g. Hutchings and Shulman, 1999). They broadly adhere to the following pattern: an opening page/section delineates briefly the aims, purpose and context of the discussion within the module in which it is located. From this, participants can move either to the task itself or to a background paper written specifically by course tutors drawing on key literature in the field and listing carefully selected, recommended background reading. The task usually offers a choice of questions as well as links to two or three digitised core readings. Participants are encouraged to read the background paper before they choose the task and to engage with the digitised readings before composing their response to the task (usually 300–500 words) by a specific date. In a further step, they are required to submit at least one additional posting by a specified date per online discussion in response to the contributions made by their peers. Usually the task page also offers a sample response authored by a course tutor as well as a sample follow-up posting for exemplification. Course tutors then summarise participants' contributions and, thereby, 'close' the discussion. The templates, therefore, provide a framework for information gathering, the stimulation of recall of prior knowledge and the guiding of knowledge construction. (Pachler, Daly and Lambert, 2003)

Parsell and Duke-Yonge (2007: 188) conceptualize their courses in the subject domain of philosophy by the notion of virtual communities of enquiry and have adopted the following template:

- Students are asked to read trigger material.

- They are asked to post a message about what they found most puzzling or interesting.
- The tutor attempts to group the questions.
- Students are then asked to discuss the grouped questions facilitated by the tutor; the tutor is asked to participate actively in the discussion by "exhibiting puzzlement, asking questions that signal the cognitive moves that might be useful and concentrating students' attention on meta-cognition ... without providing firm solutions and hold back on matters of fact"—the tutor is asked to be "pedagogically strong but philosophically self-effacing".
- The tutor should jump-start stalled discussions and encourage students to take responsibility for their comments and be "prepared to defend, modify or change them as appropriate".

Parsell and Duke-Yonge's work brings to the fore the importance of the role of the tutor and her pedagogical skills in facilitating learner interaction, collaboration and communication effectively in an online context. Work by Gilly Salmon on e-moderation (2002, 2004) has been very influential, if not uncontested, certainly in the early days of e-learning and sets out a conceptual "Five Stage Model" of effective e-moderation based on a linear model of learning along a trajectory of access and motivation, online socialization, information exchange, knowledge construction and development. Whilst the Five Stage Model has been contested, the notion of e moderation, or e-facilitation, is an important pedagogical skill in the context of online learning which tutors need to develop and learn about.

Another operationalization of templates is that developed by the London Knowledge Lab at the Institute of Education, London (Jara and Mohamad, 2007) published by the WLE Centre for Excellence.[4] Jara and Mohamad offer a series of pedagogical templates for the integration of technology into teaching and learning or, more specifically, for the integration of e-learning into face-to-face provision (see Table 4.1). The templates provide descriptions of possible models of such integration.

Table 4.1   E-learning pedagogical templates
Source: Jara and Mohamad, 2007: 7

	Name	Type	Basic description
B1	Online admin. support	Blended	Core learning activities and support are face-to-face. Administrative information (announcements, calendar), readings, materials, submission of assignments, and some support are provided online.
B2	Follow-up	Blended	Core learning activities and support are face-to-face. Additional online tasks and support are organized in between sessions as follow up or preparation for the sessions (e.g. to keep communication and focus in between sessions)
B3	Parallel	Blended	Learning activities run in parallel, some in the face-to-face sessions, others online.
B4	Face-to-face events	Blended	Core learning activities and support are online. Face-to-face events/workshops are held to initiate or wrap up online activities (e.g. at the start and half way through the course)
D1	Distance online support	Distance	Core learning activities are based around print-based distance learning materials. Student support and feedback is provided online.
D2	Online resource based	Distance	Core learning activities and support are online. Learning activities are organized around resources and materials.
D3	Online discussion based	Distance	Core learning activities and support are online. Learning activities are organized around discussions.

Table 4.2 exemplifies template B3, "Parallel", in relation to a number of course components. Jara and Mohamad's report contains a discussion and exemplification of all seven templates identified by them and as such provides useful practical guidance for planning and course design.

Table 4.2 "Parallel" template

Course component	F2F	Online	VLE tools
Content	Yes	Readings and presentations	Online repository
Learning activities	Yes	Iceberg activities Discussion/seminars around specific topics Sharing of experiences, task outputs	Discussion spaces
Communications	Yes	Frequently asked questions	Discussion spaces
Learning resources	Yes	Electronic copy of handbook / readings, presentations List of websites and other online resources Samples of student projects from previous years Glossary of important key concepts	Online repository Publishing of information online
Assessment and feedback		Submission of draft/final assignment	Online drop box
Course administration		Reminders of sessions, tasks, deadlines, assignments Announcements of events, seminars Contact information of tutors, students, administrators	Announcements Calendar Publishing of information online
Course evaluation		Student satisfaction survey	Online surveys

In Pachler and Daly (2006a) we proposed different types of "template" for online (professional) learning. Central to these templates is meta-level engagement of learners, both at a procedural as well as at a declarative level of knowing around which we developed four design principles, or templates, for online learning. They are rooted in professional online learning but we consider them to have transfer value beyond to other types of online provision:

- the narrative principle
- the discourse principle
- the argumentation principle
- the intercultural principle.

The narrative principle foregrounds the role of learner narrative with an emphasis on narrative function, rather than form. This principle is influenced heavily by Bruner's (1985) concept of narrative as a "mode of thought" that seeks explanations of the world, or ways of understanding, which are rooted in the contexts in which events occur. Narrative offers ways of understanding that are different from attempts to establish constant logico-scientific "truth". The narrative principle is rooted in Bruner's concept of "verisimilitude" or "truth-likeness" by which human beings are able to understand their experiences and engage in sense-making in order to articulate experience and make it shareable.

The discourse principle follows Turoff et al.'s (1999) notion of "conceptual discourse templates" or "domain independent general meta-discussion structures". The concept of a discourse structure as they use it is defined as "a template for a discussion structure which allows individuals to classify their contributions to the discussion into meaningful categories that structure their relevance and significance according to the nature of the topic, the objective of the discussion, and the characteristics of the group". In our practice we foreground the critical role played by texts in provoking meta-level discussion. We see relations between participants and the textual environment as instrumental in achieving critical levels of discussion, and as constantly negotiated between participants. The relations that exist between texts, the individual learner and peer discourse constitute the basis for the development of knowledge.

The argumentative principle is based on the work of Andriessen, Baker and Suthers (2003), who view argumentation as an important realization of collaborative activity, requiring learners to confront cognition. They view cognitions as representations of the mind that find articulation in points of view and so on which foreground semiotic and linguistic activity. Argumentation is seen as an epistemic activity, which involves the expression of knowledge and the relationships between aspects of knowledge.

The intercultural principle relates to the fact that the increasingly cross-cultural composition of online groups can have a significant effect on the nature and extent of the learning that takes place which needs to be taken into account and addressed explicitly pedagogically. Online learning increasingly brings together participants with different cultural backgrounds, for example, in terms of individual differences, educational histories, linguistic capabilities, cultural values and dispositions, and personal and/or professional experiences.

Different online environments develop different "cultures of use" which emerge from these influences.

In the domain of foreign language education and using the term task design rather than templates, O'Dowd and Waire (2009: 176–7) delineate twelve intercultural telecollaborative tasks, which they synthesized from the literature:

- authoring "cultural autobiographies"
- carrying out virtual interviews
- engaging in informal discussion
- exchanging story collections
- comparing parallel texts
- comparing class questionnaires
- analysing cultural products
- translating
- collaborating on product creation
- transforming text genres
- carrying out "closed outcome" discussions
- making cultural translations/adaptations.

(Aspects of) these building blocks can not only form the basis of various templates for online foreign language courses but also online provision in other subject areas.

Another type of template that can be found in the literature is called "collaboration scripts". The so-called scripts are "scaffolds that aim to improve collaboration through structuring the interactive processes between two or more learning partners" (Kollar, Fischer and Hesse, 2006: 159) and exist face-to-face and online. Collaboration scripts can be seen to consist of at least five components: (a) learning objectives, (b) type of activities, (c) sequencing, (d) role distribution and (e) type of representation. According to the research by Kollar, Fischer and Hesse (2006), scripts for computer-mediated collaboration are typically concerned with facilitating communicative-coordinative processes that occur among group members. Compared with earlier templates, the intention here is—at least to some extent—to find ways of automating collaboration through the identification of such scripts and to guide the design of discursive learning tasks.

In his attempt to outline a theory of online learning, Anderson (2008) draws on Bransford, Brown and Cocking (1999), who propose four overlapping lenses through which to examine learning environments:

- learner/learning-centred
- knowledge-centred
- community-centred
- assessment-centred.

From the perspective of a pedagogical, rather than a technological engagement with e-learning it is instructive, according to Anderson (2008: 66), to consider the affordances of new technologies in relation to these lenses and to construct a learning environment that is simultaneously learner-centred, knowledge-centred, community-centred and assessment-centred. For example, the knowledge-centred lens, according to Anderson, works on the assumption that effective learning is bound up with the context and epistemology of a discipline. From this flow a number of possible questions, such as: is the assumption that there exists a canonical body of knowledge which is to be transmitted most effectively to the learner in order to be internalized by her? Or: is knowledge viewed as something contested, fluid and situated? Depending on the perspective taken different technologies will be chosen and deployed in different ways. Ostensibly the implication is for an explicit pedagogical stance to be taken in relation to these four lenses.

Learner/learning-centredness is also a prominent feature of McCombs and Vakili's framework for e-learning (2005). For these authors, learner-centredness

> is the perspective that couples a focus on individual learners—their heredity, experiences, perspectives, backgrounds, talents, interests, capacities, and needs—with a focus on learning—the best available knowledge about learning and how it occurs and about teaching practices that are most effective in promoting the highest levels of motivation, learning, and achievement for all learners. (p. 1584)

Interestingly, and importantly from an implementation perspective, McCombs and Vakili do not view learner-centredness as operating at the micro-level of instructional practices or the meso-level of programmes and courses alone; they stress that it exists in the complex interaction of the micro- with the meso- and the macro-level of policies. They argue the need for an e-learning framework and for such a framework not only to be research-based, that is, to draw on existing research findings, but also research validated, that is, to have been empirically tested and proven (p. 1583). They propose the 14 principles of the American Psychological Association Work Group of the Board of Educational Affairs (1997) as foundational (see Figure 4.1) and delineate a wide range of implications for practice from them (see McCombs and Vakili, 2005: 1591–5). McCombs and Vakili, therefore, posit psychological principles as bases for e-learning design.

Cognitive and metacognitive factors

Principle 1: Nature of the learning process

The learning of complex subject matter is most effective when it is an intentional process of constructing meaning from information and experience.

Principle 2: Goals of the learning process

The successful learner, over time and with support and instructional guidance, can create meaningful, coherent representations of knowledge.

Principle 3: Construction of knowledge

The successful learner can link new information with existing knowledge in meaningful ways.

Principle 4: Strategic thinking

The successful learner can create and use a repertoire of thinking and reasoning strategies to achieve complex learning goals.

Principle 5: Thinking about thinking

Higher order strategies for selecting and monitoring mental operations facilitate creative and critical thinking.

Principle 6: Context of learning

Learning is influenced by environmental factors, including culture, technology, and instructional practices.

Motivational and affective factors

Principle 7: Motivational and emotional influences on learning

What and how much is learned is influenced by the learner's motivation. Motivation to learn, in turn, is influenced by the individual's emotional states, beliefs, interests and goals and habits of thinking.

Principle 8: Intrinsic motivation to learn

The learner's creativity, higher order thinking and natural curiosity all contribute to motivation to learn. Intrinsic motivation is stimulated by tasks of optimal novelty and difficulty, relevant to personal interests, and providing for personal choice and control.

Principle 9: Effects of motivation on effort

Acquisition of complex knowledge and skills requires extended learner effort and guided practice. Without the learner's motivation to learn, the willingness to exert this effort is unlikely without coercion.

Developmental and social factors

Principle 10: Developmental influences on learning

As individuals develop, they encounter different opportunities for and experience different constraints on learning. Learning is most effective when differential development within and across physical, intellectual, emotional, and social domains is taken into account.

Principle 11: Social influences on learning

Learning is influenced by social interactions, interpersonal relations and communication with others.

Individual-differences factors

Principle 12: Individual differences in learning

Learners have different strategies, approaches and capabilities for learning that are a function of prior experience and heredity.

Principle 13: Learning and diversity

Learning is most effective when differences in learners' linguistic, cultural and social backgrounds are taken into account.

Principle 14: Standards and assessment

Setting appropriately high and challenging standards and assessing the learner and learning progress—including diagnostic, process and outcome assessment—are integral parts of the learning process.

Figure 4.1   Learner-centred psychological principles
Source: McCombs and Vakili, 2005: 1585–6

Anderson proposes the following model of e-learning (see Figure 4.2) which illustrates learners and teachers and their interactions with each other and with the content.

The model suggests a range of interactions (student–teacher, student–student, student–content), which can be variously operationalized according to local context. Anderson (2008: 66) argues that the various forms of student interaction can be substituted with each other without there being a decrease in the quality of learning. At least one form of interaction needs to be present at a high level he posits.

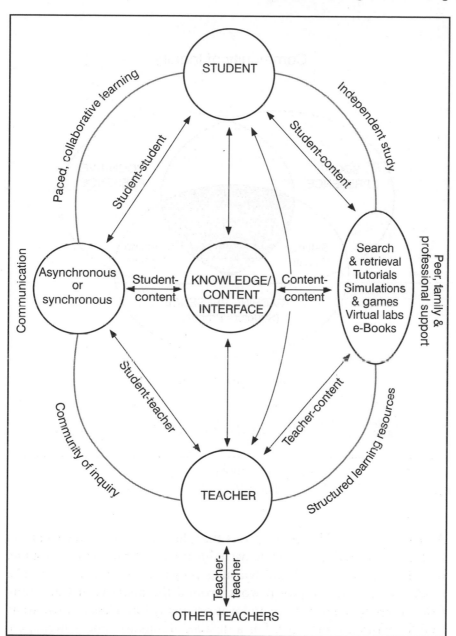

Figure 4.2 A model of e-learning
Source: Anderson, 2008: 61

One popular conceptual framework explaining the online learning experience is the so-called community of inquiry model first developed by Garrison, Anderson and Archer (2000; see also Garrison and

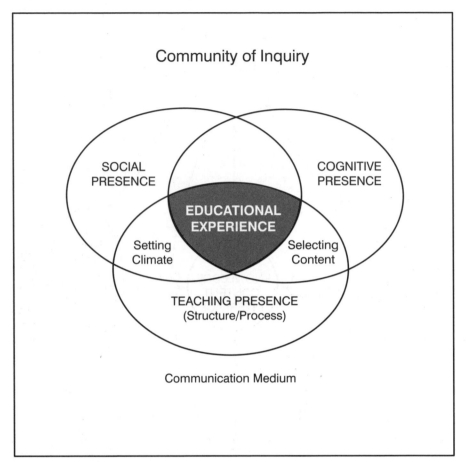

Figure 4.3   Community of inquiry model
Source: http://communitiesofinquiry.com/files/coi_model.pdf

Anderson, 2003). The model posits that there exist three key elements that are essential to an effective educational "transaction" online, namely cognitive, social and teaching presence (see Figure 4.3). The model is based on empirical work around the analysis of transcripts from computer-conferencing and was originally intended as an analysis tool for written transcripts. For a detailed discussion and critique, see e.g. Daly, 2008b.

Cognitive presence is understood as the extent to which learners are able to construct meaning through sustained communication. Social presence is the ability of learners to project their personal characteristics into the community. And teaching presence is defined as the design, facilitation and direction of cognitive and social processes for the purpose of realizing educational outcomes (see Garrison, Anderson and Archer, 2000). The model sets out a number of categories and indicators within each of these three elements around how online communication and discourse can facilitate higher-order thinking skills which can be taken as proxies for learning (Table 4.3). We offer it here together with the other models as a possible planning tool for online pedagogical interventions and argue that it presents a useful checklist for planning online teaching episodes. Joop van Schie developed a useful and detailed concept map based on the community of inquiry that lends itself very well to planning as it describes the three presences of the community of inquiry model in concrete terms.[6]

For the purposes of this chapter we wish to present one final model of learning, namely that developed by Conole and Fill (2005; Figure 4.4) which also lends itself to planning at various levels as well as to analysing and deconstructing practice.

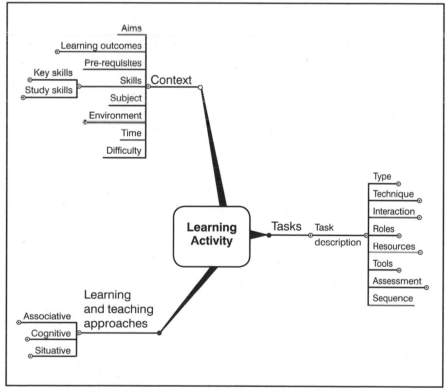

Figure 4.4 Conole and Fill's model of learning
Source: Conole and Fill, 2005: 8

Table 4.3 Community of inquiry categories
Source: Vaughan and Garrison, 2007: 142

Elements	Categories	Indicators
Social presence	Affective expression Open communication Group cohesion	Emoticons Express trust, agreement Encourage collaboration
Teaching presence	Design and organization Facilitating discourse Direct instruction	Defining content and activities Sharing meaning Focusing discussion
Cognitive presence	Triggering event Exploration Integration Resolution	Sense of puzzlement Information exchange Connecting ideas Apply new ideas

Readers will have noticed that the templates, models and frameworks we have introduced here—despite them not having been analysed in detail due to the summary intentions of this chapter—are rather different in approach, level of granularity and scope and so on. They represent differing interests of researchers, theorists and practitioners, and clearly the range of templates/models continues to be developed. It is important to acknowledge that categorizing these models offers a useful way to navigate the territory. Conole and Oliver (2002), for example, differentiate between:

- frameworks: which define concepts and can be used as a specialized language for the discussion of design issues;
- models: which relate concepts and can be processed based or analytic;
- toolkits: which provide structured processes to support decision-making; and
- software wizards: which support automated design.

Given the level of generality of our discussion and in line with our intention to provide an overview, a more nuanced differentiation is not included here. A cautionary lesson is offered by de Freitas et al. (2007) in terms of the applicability of delineated e-learning "models" to new pedagogical contexts. Their study introduced a group of practitioners to a model for the purposes of relating it to their own practice and eliciting their reflections on it. The study confirmed previous findings whereby un-mediated exposure to such models did not lead to understanding, engagement or impact irrespective of how good they are conceptually and/or technically (p. 29). The relationship with practitioners' own practice needs to be supported. One reason for that is often a gap in the abstraction of the model and what it is trying to represent (p. 32). Lack of clarity of terminology also often becomes a critical issue (p. 33). As a result we want to stress that there appears to be little merit in attempting to design a "universal" approach that synthesizes the key features of the various models as that, according to de Freitas et al.'s work is undesirable from a practitioner perspective or impossible in the sense that practitioners will invariably perceive the need for adaptation at the expense of standardization.

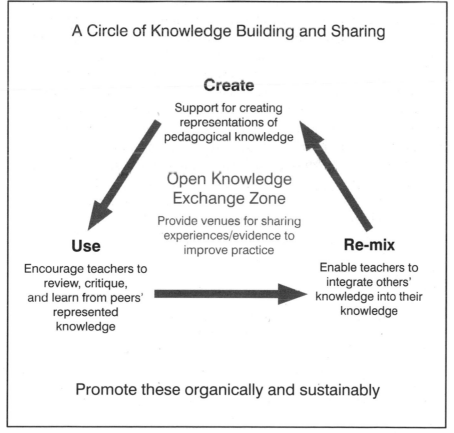

Figure 4.5   A circle of knowledge building and sharing
Source: Brown and Adler, 2008: 28

Conclusion

We wish to conclude this chapter with a brief look at the implications of Brown and Adler's (2008) notion of "learning to be" (see Figure 4.5). In Pachler, Bachmair and Cook (2010) we discuss this phenomenon in the context of what we call the "outside in–inside out" challenge of mobile devices: the provision of learning opportunities in a world dominated by ubiquitous internet access is no longer the preserve of institutions of learning but instead dispersed across innumerable virtual and real sites providing mediated and un-mediated content and opportunities for meaning-making in and of the world. Attendant to this change in location is a change in structures and processes represented by Brown and Adler in Figure 4.5.

One of the challenges, therefore, for e-learning offered by educational institutions such as universities is to "compete" with what is available outside the confines of their walled gardens and to provide opportunities to students for meaningful, reflective, responsible and "effective" use of this dynamic infrastructure as well as the students' own (social networks) and to bring it and the attendant processes into a fruitful relationship with what is on offer in-house. Models and frameworks for e-learning, although captured and analysed within the "academy", continue to evolve and be identified by forces, social, cultural and technological, beyond the institutions which seek to understand and harness them. The challenge of "learning to be" within this context applies to all those who teach and learn, and also to those who develop policy, nationally and institutionally, aimed at bringing about a sustainable interface between technological and pedagogical developments.

Notes

1 http://blip.tv/file/2718176.
2 http://www.jisc.ac.uk/publications/documents/llpfinal.aspx.
3 http://www.jisc.ac.uk/whatwedo/programmes/ elearningpedagogy/phoebe.aspx.
4 http://www.wlecentre.ac.uk.
5 http://communitiesofinquiry.com/files/concept-map.gif.

e-Assessment, e-Portfolios, Quality Assurance and the Student Experience $\boxed{5}$

Chapter Outline

Introduction	109
Quality assurance and the student experience	109
e-Assessment	111
Some examples of e-assessment practices	119
e-Portfolios	122
Conclusion	126

Introduction

This chapter is underpinned by notions of student self-regulation and ownership of the learning experience and of knowledge-making processes. The various aspects of e-assessment, e-portfolios and quality assurance included here have a common concern with meta-learning processes and the role played by technologies in enhancing learner participation in assessment approaches. E-assessment and its related concerns are viewed as integral to new literate and cultural learning practices.

Quality assurance and the student experience

Closely linked to the discussion of online learning and teaching in Chapter 4 is the need to assure the quality of the student experience as an e-learner. The drivers for quality assurance and enhancement are manifold: they relate on the one hand *inter alia* to notions of competitiveness in an international education market and value for money for consumers—assuming one accepts the neo-liberal view of education—as well as, of course, an important factor in relation to learner motivation and success (see e.g. Muilenburg and Berge, 2005) and as such of great importance for us. Evaluation of online provision, be it technology-enhanced face-to-face, mixed mode or online, therefore, must be seen as an integral part of teaching and learning and we consider the role of the learner in the process of evaluation as central. In Daly et al. (2007) we proposed an evaluation strategy that is "embedded" or built into the course design process and focuses on the subjective and perceptual aspect of the e-learner's experience. Evaluation strategies aim to elicit learner narratives, so that learners articulate and reflect on the processes they engage with at a meta-level. This can be by "storying" about their experiences, engaging with "thinking aloud" in response to stimuli or online group talk about their learning. Compared with proposals by some in the field (see e.g. Rovai, 2003: 112, who distinguishes objectives-, management-, consumer-, expertise-, adversary- and participant-orientated evaluation strategies), we explore a research-based approach, drawing on narrative methods, which aims at understanding and recognizing e-learners' experiences as social practice. E-learners are acknowledged as participating in complex and dynamic processes which take place over time. There are shortcomings in evaluation approaches which focus solely on satisfaction at particular points in the process, normally upon completion, or 'impact' against a specific set of (predetermined) criteria or measures (Rovai, 2003: 444).

Narrative evaluation approaches can be seen to address findings from research, such as those carried out by Jara and Mellar (2010), which suggest that in the context of e-learning traditional strategies for collecting student feedback—module evaluations and student representation—are both strongly affected by the distinctive features of the mode of delivery in e-learning and, as a consequence, not able to adequately support quality enhancement. Jara and Mellar found that the remote location of the students impacts on student representation as well as on the response rates for module evaluations. The enhancement function of module evaluations, therefore, can be seen to be "adversely affected by lack of appropriate course management arising from the disaggregation of course processes and the resulting ambiguity in the allocation of responsibilities" (p. 1).

Jara and Mellar (2010: 3) identify four important factors why there is a need of adapting approaches in evaluation compared with face-to-face provision:

- disaggregated processes: in e-learning courses the processes involved (e.g. design, delivery, assessment) are often the responsibility of separate teams, in contrast with conventional face-to-face courses where these tasks are responsibility of one team;
- distribution of teams: academic staff do not work in isolation, staff need to work collaboratively, interacting with other professionals, and in the case of e-learning courses these people may well be located in different sites;
- distant location of students: staff have less direct access to students than with campus-based learning; and
- openness to review: in e-learning courses student (and tutor) activities in using technology for learning can be monitored in greater depth and more continuously and unobtrusively than in campus-based learning or traditional distance learning.

The underpinning evaluation perspective is concerned with meta-level engagement with learning. Our approach is premised on learning being enhanced through students' awareness of their own learning identities, "by which capacities for learning and developing practice are rooted explicitly in autobiographical dimensions of growth and transformation" (Jara and Mellar, 2010: 445). Such evaluation, namely one that is embedded or concurrent with the process of studying, can establish a reciprocal relationship between tutors and students around how the learning is going. It foregrounds the need for

> meta-level engagement of students with their learning, and for tools by which they explicitly explore and understand the processes of being an e-learner and the altered ways of thinking and practising that are demanded. (p. 445)

e-Assessment

As already discussed in Chapter 1, self-regulation can be considered to be an important aspect of the learning process; it refers to the control by students of aspects of their own learning. In the context of this chapter the question arises to what extent technology-enhanced assessment might support and foster self-regulation.

Nicol and Macfarlane-Dick (2006: x) identified seven principles of good feedback practice from the research literature that might help support learner self-regulation. In later work, Nicol (2007: 3) extended this to 10 (see Figure 5.1).

Good assessment and feedback practices should:

1. Help clarify what good performance is (goals, criteria, standards).

   To what extent do students in your course have opportunities to engage actively with goals, criteria and standards, before, during and after an assessment task?

2. Encourage "time and effort" on challenging learning tasks.

   To what extent do your assessment tasks encourage regular study in and out of class and deep rather than surface learning?

3. Deliver high-quality feedback information that helps learners self-correct.

   What kind of teacher feedback do you provide—in what ways does it help students self-assess and self-correct?

4. Encourage positive motivational beliefs and self-esteem.

   To what extent do your assessments and feedback processes activate your students' motivation to learn and be successful?

5. Encourage interaction and dialogue around learning (peer and teacher–student).

   What opportunities are there for feedback dialogue (peer and/or tutor–student) around assessment tasks in your course?

6. Facilitate the development of self-assessment and reflection in learning.

   To what extent are there formal opportunities for reflection, self-assessment or peer assessment in your course?

7. Give learners choice in assessment—content and processes

   To what extent do students have choice in the topics, methods, criteria, weighting and/or timing of learning and assessment tasks in your course?

8. Involve students in decision-making about assessment policy and practice.

   To what extent are your students in your course kept informed or engaged in consultations regarding assessment decisions?

9. Support the development of learning communities

To what extent do your assessments and feedback processes help support the development of learning communities?

10. Help teachers adapt teaching to student needs

To what extent do your assessment and feedback processes help inform and shape your teaching?

Figure 5.1   Good assessment and feedback practices
Source: Nicol, 2007: 3

Nicol and Milligan (2006) examine the role technology can play in supporting these principles and raise a number of important issues for consideration.

In relation to helping students achieve an understanding about what constitutes good performance they note that simply publishing assessment criteria in a virtual learning environment tends to be insufficient, particularly for complex tasks. They recommend additional strategies such as an online discussion about the criteria as well as the provision of examples of completed tasks and a requirement for students to analyse them and think about which criteria they meet and how.

In relation to the principle concerning reflection and self-assessment students might be required to do the same in relation to their own work and that of peers. The construction of an e-portfolio, discussed in more detail later, is another way of engaging students in reflection about their own learning at a meta-level.

One important challenge in the context of e-learning exists around the provision of tutor feedback to scaffold the development of learner self-regulation. In order to offer scaffolding, tutor feedback needs to provide information about the gap between student performance and the learning goals and such information is invariably bound up with the need to provide specific advice as well as, according to research, descriptive rather than evaluative information (see Wiggins, 2001). Nicol and Milligan (2006) suggest the use of databanks of feedback comments grounded in educational principles as an important way forward. One such principle might be Lunsford's (1997) reader-response strategy in which tutor comments aim to help students grasp the difference between intentions and effects of writing by playing back to the student how an essay worked from the tutor's perspective and by giving corrective advice rather than just information about strengths and weaknesses. Clearly, such approaches to the provision of feedback are highly individualized with limited scope for the use of technology for automatization.

A key issue about feedback according to Nicol and Milligan (2006) is whether or not students understand the feedback they are given. Their reading of the literature suggests that this is often not the case and that, therefore, students are not able to internalize and apply it. One possible way of addressing this shortcoming, they suggest, is to conceptualize feedback as a dialogic process to which technology can contribute, for example through what they call "class-wide discussion" in which student responses and reasoning behind their answers are collated and played back to students as a basis for peer discussion.

Work by Black and Wiliam (1998) shows that feedback can have an important effect on motivation and self-esteem, which in turn affect what and how students learn. Technology-enhanced assessment can allow students to engage more with their own learning against external criteria as opposed to norm-referenced comparisons to their peers. The ability to more easily revisit records of their own learning process and its outcomes, including feedback received, is considered to be an important contribution of technology to the assessment process.

One particular challenge in online courses, most notably where assessment comprises mainly summative written coursework is the ability for students to act upon feedback received and "close the gap" between current and optimal understanding, for example, by revising their drafts of coursework or having the opportunity to apply the advice received to future pieces of work.

This challenge also pertains to the ability of tutors to act upon the implications of the feedback given to students about their own teaching and course design. In order for both students and tutors to be able to feed forward the insights gained through assessment activities into their learning and teaching, it seems important to build into the course design formative, diagnostic and self-assessment opportunities.

For a detailed discussion of formative e-assessment, see Pachler et al. (2009) and Pachler et al. (2010). In this body of work, which emerged in the context of a JISC-funded study, formative e-assessment is defined as the use of ICT to support the iterative process of gathering and analysing information about student learning by teachers as well as learners and of evaluating it in relation to prior achievement and attainment of intended, as well as unintended learning outcomes. Within this definition, technologies of e-assessment are not seen as in themselves being inherently either summative or formative, but rather what is of interest is whether e-assessment is being used summatively or formatively. This is in line with a socio-technical view of educational systems, which sees the technological dimensions (e.g. speed, storage capacity, processing, communication, construction and representation and mutability) as inseparable from the pedagogical parameters (e.g. verbal/electronic/synchronous/asynchronous interaction between key players which brings about changes in concepts or skills).

Our research into formative assessment (Pachler et al., 2009: 4–5) has clearly shown, that the "e" has a significant contribution to add to assessment, in particular:

Speed
- Speed of response is often important in enabling feedback to have an effect.
- Supports rapid iteration—the ability to give feedback quickly means that the student's next problem solving iteration can begin more quickly.

Storage capacity
- Ability to access very large amounts of data (so appropriate feedback/additional work/illustrations can be identified).

Processing
- Automation—in some situations the e-assessment system can analyse responses automatically and provide appropriate feedback.
- Scalability—can often be the result of some level of automation.
- Adaptivity—systems can adapt to students.

Communication
- Often the advantage of the "e" is that it enables rapid communication of ideas across a range of audiences, and the technology allows this range to be controlled, it can be just one person, a group, a class or more.
- This communication aspect means that aspects of communication can be captured and given a degree of semi-permanence.
- This semi-permanence supports the sharing of intellectual objects.

Construction and representation
- Representation—the ability to represent ideas in a variety of ways and to move and translate between these representations.
- Technology can support learners in the representation of their own ideas.

- Through representation technology enables concepts to be "shaped" and this helps learners develop their meaning.
- In representing their ideas in digital artefacts learners open up a window on their thinking.

Mutability

- Shared objects are not fixed, they can change/be changed easily.

It is consistent with a view of learning as "conversational", and this range of combined resources impacts not only on how students act but also informs what teachers do to enhance learning.

Following Black and Wiliam (2009), we propose the concept of "moments of contingency": critical points in the teaching and learning process where the flow of instruction cannot be predetermined as a key concept. Moments of contingency contain within them the scope for learners' understanding to be "otherwise". The technology itself does not create these moments: they are dependent on teachers' and learners' actions. But for technology to perform formatively, it needs to acknowledge and support these moments. Clearly, moments of contingency pose a key pedagogical and design challenge in the context of online learning.

Of particular potential also, from our perspective, is the potential of digital technology in relation to representation, the ability to represent ideas in a variety of ways to move and translate between these representations. The digital artefacts produced by learners can be seen to open up a window for tutors on students' thinking. For example, a digital photograph which is taken to capture a particular instance of practice or example of learning can inform a tutor's awareness of how a student is approaching a particular task. Consequently, we would encourage a wide range of representational options to be designed into online learning experiences.

In Figure 5.2 we feature a word cloud as one example of how the information contained in this chapter can be represented differently through the affordances of digital technologies. Figure 5.2 offers a visual shorthand to readers. It might be instructive as an "at-a-glance" overview of the key themes covered in the chapter and could be used by readers of the book to make decisions about whether or not to read and engage with the chapter in the first place. As such it can be seen as a possible alternative to an abstract and makes certain judgments and inferences possible. It also vividly underscores the relative importance of the themes and, by implication, allows inferences about the authorial stance taken.

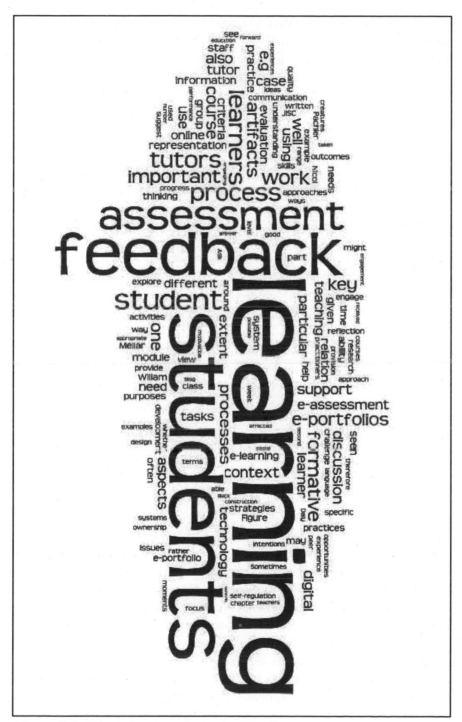

Figure 5.2   Word cloud created using Wordle
Source: http://www.wordle.net

Our approach to formative e-assessment draws centrally on recent work by Black and Wiliam (2009: 8), which conceptualizes formative assessment in terms of five key strategies:

1. engineering effective classroom discussion, questions and learning tasks that elicit evidence of learning;
2. providing feedback that moves learners forward;
3. clarifying and sharing learning intentions and criteria for success;
4. activating students as owners of their own learning;
5. activating students as instructional resources for one another;

and posits the key aspects of formative assessment in Table 5.1.

Table 5.1 Key aspects of formative assessment
Source: Black and Wiliam, 2009: 8

	Where the learner is going	Where the learner is	How to get there
Teacher	Clarify and share learning intentions	Engineering effective discussions, tasks and activities that elicit evidence of learning	Providing feedback that moves learners forward
Peer	Understand and share learning intentions	Activating learners as learning resources for one another	
Learner	Understand learning intentions	Activating learners as owners of their own learning	

These "key aspects" assume that assessment is bound up with the social relations of the learning context and that these aspects may have widely varying feedback cycles in terms of the time and people involved. Essentially, learner ownership of their learning, understanding and actions is implied here. With e-learning, this is facilitated by the socio-technical view of educational systems outlined above, which sees the technological dimensions (e.g. speed, storage capacity, processing, communication, construction and representation and mutability) as inseparable from the pedagogical parameters (e.g. verbal/electronic/synchronous/asynchronous interaction between key players which brings about changes in concepts or skills).

Some examples of e-assessment practices

We explored Black and Wiliam's "key aspects" as part of the JISC project on formative e-assessment (Pachler et al., 2009), where we invited practitioners to face-to-face meetings where we prompted them to recount their experiences of using formative e-assessment as case stories and to discuss these with their peers. The construction and discussion of these narratives were scaffolded by a set of tools which captured the accounts of practice which were elicited through collaborative activities. We present here some examples of cases, named by the participants, to illustrate the nature, type and scope of some of the work being undertaken by tutors in higher education. More detail about the project and the cases can be found at http://www.snipurl.com/feasst.

Audiofiles

Audiofiles have been piloted with 25 undergraduate university students in years 1, 2 and 3 in a school of sociology and social policy. They form part of ongoing research and development to improve strategies for tutors to give feedback to students on traditional written essays to help deal with a contemporary challenge—increasing class sizes and less time for staff to spend on feedback on written coursework, leading to inconsistency in feedback even where it is done well. The intervention sought to explore the value of replacing text-based feedback with audio feedback, and to find out "Does the feedback change?" Tutors used both handheld dictaphones and audio software to record their feedback directly onto a PC. There were no rules about the length of the file. Feedback was recorded in a single audiofile at the conclusion to reading the whole piece of writing and lasted between 90 seconds and 21 minutes. Audiofiles were then returned to the students via the VLE (Blackboard). The research found that tutors tended to comment more freely than in their equivalent written feedback which tended to conform more closely to the content guidelines of a feedback template sheet. It appears that the nature of the feedback may be affected by the use of audiofiles. Comments were "richer" and more emphatic which may affect student motivation. In comparing the audio transcripts with written feedback from the same tutors, the feedback tended to be richer, longer, personalized, more immediate and "authentic". The process appeared to make tutors reflect more on their own feedback and this led to the desire to amend it. It takes tutors longer to produce however, and further development may help the staff with managing this.

The student work was also being formally assessed, so the students were getting formative outcomes from a summative piece of work, and the approach may be more effective in a purely formative context. Next steps will be to: explore audiofiles with other disciplines; explore the possibilities of inserting feedback at intervals into the body of the documents like "comment" inserts on word files; enable tutors to easily edit the word files as they make them.

Como

At the Royal Veterinary College, a group of students were engaged in practical work in a vet training hospital. As part of their training, the students were required to capture instances of practice on a mobile phone and the photos collected were automatically uploaded to flickr. The students worked in groups of 4 or 5 and each was provided with a mobile phone and given a short familiarization session. In one scenario, during morning rounds students would be directed to monitor the progress of an animal being treated. Their task would be to document case progress over time. They took pictures throughout the day, uploaded them to a blog, tagged them with caseID and key features, such as type of animal, the injury, condition. The students then used quiet moments to add details to the "case" using blog postings. During the evening rounds, the students presented their cases in group discussion sessions with their tutor, using the images, blog posts and a projector. The group reviewed the diagnosis and the actions which were taken in the light of revisiting the images and postings which acted as catalysts for evaluation of practice. Co-reflection was enhanced because of the availability of images which bring the medical case into the seminar room. It affected the students' tutorial conversation, providing ongoing formative contributions to the case in the form of postings. The discussion moved from abstract "textbook theory" to what tutors called "case presentation": how the particular condition presents itself in a particular case, how to analyse symptoms in real-world conditions and how to assess treatment. These are key skills which are often neglected due to the inability to have a concrete presence of the case in the seminar room as a focus for reflective and analytical discussion. The process of using images to capture cases also provided feedback to tutors on the students' learning. Tutors reported that observing students' pictures gave them a window on their thinking: what they noticed, where their attention was and where they assigned importance. This was the basis for modifying tutor input and the focus of the tutorial discussion.

Creature of the week

A large class (138) of first- and second-year computer science students took part in a programming module called Interactive Systems. The students' assignment was to create a virtual pet in Second Life. This involves 3D-modelling and programming skills. The intended effect was to engage and motivate the students, to show examples of good work which others could learn from and show students their work is valued. It was also an aim to build a sense of community among such a large group. The approach was to introduce "creature of the week". This means that the tutor selected a virtual pet from the Second Life island every week, took a screen shot of it, and displayed that screenshot at the start of every lecture. It also went on the class blog in the VLE for the module. Sometimes there were runner-up creatures. The students liked seeing the creatures, and the owner of the creature was often sheepishly proud. Sometimes students informed the tutor that someone's pet should be creature of the week, sometimes they suggested that theirs should be chosen. They also pointed out good examples they had seen which had not been showcased and thought it was important that students were not excluded by their creature being overlooked for showcasing. The tutor enjoyed doing this and highlighted the importance of tutors engaging in "fun" activities. It is a "light weight" way of trying to create a fun class community. It works because the assignment is about something visual, and because the project was ongoing for 12 weeks so momentum could build around the choice each week. In a similar vein, at a Virtual Crufts at the end of semester, peer nominated creatures get prizes.

Sometimes the tutor did a live demo of the creatures in Second Life to show interactive behaviour. Sometimes she chose creatures which display particular techniques the group has been learning about. Sometimes she picked them because they appeal to her.

String Comparison

Undergraduates can take Spanish as an optional module while studying other subjects at a UK university and the module grade counts towards the final degree. The students need to practise written language independently and receive feedback on errors in order to improve their language skills. There are large numbers of students taking the module making it time-consuming for tutors to provide detailed individual feedback. Standard parser-based solutions were not feasible since these tend not to be able to cope in the face of poor answers, so a bespoke string (sequence) comparator was designed. Rather than using parsing the system uses fine-granularity sequence comparison to compare correct language strings to a user's answer. With such a technique generic—but detailed—feedback is always given, no matter how confused the user's answer is. Students answer randomly generated, translation-based questions, grouped into exercises on specific areas of grammar. The comparator marks up errors in their input using colour coding (and font style) to highlight the different types of error: incorrect words, misspelt or misconjugated words, omitted words, redundant words and incorrect word-order. The student is given a second attempt in which to correct the submission based on the feedback received. The sequence comparator is language-independent and feedback is therefore generic in nature (i.e. no specific grammatical clues are given), but this was considered preferable to using a system which would not be able to handle muddled input. Despite the lack of grammatical information in the feedback the system works very well. There is virtually always an improvement between students' first and second answer attempts; but there is also measurable improvement over the course of an exercise. The system sets a minimum and maximum number of questions to be attempted for each exercise. Students can stop after completing the minimum, but can carry on to the maximum if they wish. On average students attempted 50 per cent more questions than they were required to do. As students progress through an exercise their answers become more accurate while their thinking time decreases which is an indication of improvement in language learning capacity.

e-Portfolios

The purposes of e-portfolios are various: one key question is whether the collection of artefacts in electronic form is primarily for assessment purposes, for example, demonstrating a student's abilities or documenting his/her learning journey, or whether it is viewed as a tool for shared ownership of digital artefacts between students, tutors, institutions and the wider world (Clark and Neumann, 2009). Barrett (2004) distinguished the following purposes for e-portfolios:

- as assessment tools to document the attainment of standards (a positivist model—the assessment portfolio);
- as digital stories of deep learning (a constructivist model— the learning or process portfolio); and
- as digital resumes to highlight competence (a showcase model—the best works/marketing/employment portfolio).

She notes that these purposes are in tension with each other. From this follows that there are issues around one portfolio fulfilling multiple purposes. We find the JISC (2008a: 6) definition of e-portfolios helpful in this context: it conceptualizes e-portfolios in terms of process and product and views the product as purposeful aggregation by the learner of digital artefacts articulating aspects of learning in a repository. The process JISC considers e-portfolios to be characterized by an engagement in planning, synthesizing, sharing, discussing, reflecting, giving, receiving and responding to feedback. In this context a number of variables can be seen to come into play: the degree of structure, the degree of description versus analysis, reflection and interpretation, and the extent to which the material selected is meant to be representative of a larger body of work or should exemplify accomplishments at the highest level or privacy and ownership. In order to enable the purposing and repurposing of digital artefacts evidencing or exemplifying learning for different purposes we propose the terminological distinction between an electronic repository, that is, a place where the artefacts are stored, and their presentation as e-portfolios according to different purposes. In this way duplication and confusion can be avoided and the purposing and repurposing of the artefacts can be tailored to specific needs and requirements and supported by an authoring environment and templates for structuring the artefacts. Export functions to and import functions from other systems seem as important as the need for the system to cope with multimedia artefacts.

According to Butler (2006: 3), who conducted a literature review on (e-)portfolios, the benefits of e-portfolios include that they:

- yield evidence of learning
- help to focus student thinking and facilitate reflection
- document a learner's progress over time
- develop and enhance students' communication and (organizational) skills
- provide a way of identifying and recognizing prior learning

In summary, students gain a broader sense of what they are learning, can see their learning unfolding, acquire an awareness of their accomplishments and come to understand how their learning takes place.

Attwell (2005) distinguishes seven functions of e-portfolios which should inform planning to adopt e-portfolios taken:

1. recognising learning
2. recording learning

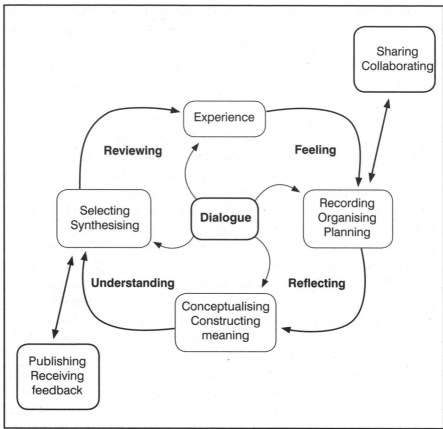

Figure 5.3 A model of e-portfolio based learning
Source: JISC, 2008a: 9

3. reflecting on learning
4. validating learning
5. presenting learning
6. planning learning
7. assessing learning.

In their report, JISC (2008a: 8–9) proposes the notion of portfolio-based learning in which students develop an improved understanding of the self and the curriculum through engagement, personalization and reflective practice. We have noted our scepticism about the proliferation of prefixes in relation to learning already in Chapter 1. Yet, we feel that Figure 5.3 helpfully exemplifies the ways in which e-portfolios can be used to support central aspects of teaching and learning.

At an operational level, JISC (2008a: 36–7) proposes six steps to e-portfolio-based learning (we prefer to think of them in terms of e-portfolio use in teaching and for learning):

1. Define—e-Portfolios can mean different things in different contexts. Establish the purpose and objectives of your e-portfolio initiative. Define the issues it aims to address, the likely support needs of the learners and the nature of the learning environment before asking: "Which tools, systems or approaches should we adopt?"

2. Understand—e-Portfolio-based learning offers real potential for autonomous and personalized learning. However, a vision for e-portfolios as the hub of student learning will have an impact on pedagogic and other institutional practices. Ask: "What kind of learning outcomes do we require from the e-portfolio initiative and what implications will this have for our practitioners, administrative and technical staff?"

3. Prepare—e-Portfolios raise a number of fundamental issues around ownership of data and identity and access management. The embedding of any e-learning tool requires assessment of risks as well as benefits, plus investment in staff training and support. Accessibility, IPR [Intellectual Property Rights], copyright and other potential legal issues also need to be raised. Ask: "Who will prepare the ground?"

4. Engage—e-Portfolio use is a far-reaching initiative that may involve practitioners, personal tutors, administrative, technical and learning support staff and, potentially, workplace mentors outside the institution. Ask: "What are the most effective strategies for engaging and sustaining the commitment of learners and those involved in supporting learners' use of e-portfolios?"

5. Implement—effective e-portfolio use does not occur on any scale without leadership from curriculum managers and practitioner teams. Ask: "What are the lessons learnt from the pilots we have run? What are the factors, such as timing or involvement of e-portfolio champions, that might influence the outcomes?"

6. Review—use a range of methodologies to explore the viewpoints both of learners and practitioners. Ask: "How will we evidence and evaluate the outcomes?"

Conclusion

Assessment plays an important part in the learning process; it informs progress and guides teaching and learning. It is important, therefore, that due consideration is given to the best possible use of the affordances of digital technologies in relation to the assessment process, for example, in terms of its validity, reliability, fairness and flexibility. Arguably there has been too much emphasis on plagiarism, that is, on the infringement of intellectual property of others by using artefacts created by others without due acknowledgement of the source. We have not focused on this issue here and suggest that, too often, the focus is concentrated on sanctions rather than on learning about attendant issues regarding the notion that language is owned by a speaker/writer. We suggest there is a need for an analysis of the causes of plagiarism for example, in relation to different academic cultures, in particular in the context of increasingly heterogeneous groups of students. Also, we view the affordance of "copy and paste" as part of a fundamental change in the cultural techniques normally referred to as literacy (see e.g. Pachler, Bachmair and Cook, 2010):

- The relationship between producers and users of artifacts is becoming increasingly blurred.
- The relationship of the user with the cultural artefacts they engage with in the process of knowledge production is frequently one of re-use underpinned by a fundamentally different attitude towards text, that is, text as open, instead of fixed, and subject to constant modifications as well as text as comprising different modalities to be (re)contextualized according to specific situational requirements.
- "Text" making is being governed by new practices, aesthetics, ethics and epistemologies.
- Text-making in this context needs to be understood as semiotic (form as content), cognitive (content as concepts) and affective (reflecting on interest and personal investment).

These characteristics pose a challenge to practitioners and designers alike to develop appropriate assessment opportunities.

We would argue that in view of the significant impact of social software on practices of use, the education system needs to be prepared for a recognition of the impact of changes in medium and mode, such as (see Australian Flexible Learning Network, 2004: 6):

- how to measure participation in online discussions and activities;
- how to measure individual performance within group assignments; and
- authentication of student work and engaging with students imaginatively.

Researching e-Learning

Chapter Outline

Introduction   129
Maturation of e-learning research   130
Researching the learning in e-learning   135
The "narrative turn"   138
The Qualitative Content Analysis model   141
Where next?   143
The theory–practice challenge for e-learning research 145

Introduction

In many ways e-learning can be said to possess many of the attributes that might be expected of an established research field. A mature infrastructure supports a range of academic practices including scholarly activity, theory-building, empirical research and dissemination, aimed at both furthering understanding and influencing policy-making across the education sectors. This is evidenced by a corpus of refereed e-learning journals,[1] international conferences[2] and dedicated bodies whose role includes the funding, brokering and dissemination of research into e-learning, which in the UK has included the Economic and Social Research Council's *Teaching and Learning Research Programme: Technology Enhanced Learning* (TLRP–TEL),[3] the Joint Information Systems Committee (JISC)[4] and the Observatory on Borderless Higher Education[5] to name but a few. Researchers across all education sectors, from primary years and secondary school sectors, informal learning, higher education and across a range of disciplines from psychology to computer science, media and cultural studies are represented within such an infrastructure.

Such forums for research have a particular focus on meta-level awareness of the evolution of the field and of the interdisciplinary backgrounds of researchers into e-learning, many of whom have migrated from other established academic disciplines. It is natural that those who engage with e-learning research should be interested in what this field actually *is* and what approaches are appropriate to understanding such a rapidly changing phenomenon which bridges social sciences, cultural theory, computer science, psychology and more. E-learning conference themes frequently include a future perspective focused on sustainability, globalization and inclusion, reflecting an imperative within the research community to understand the impact of technologies on people's lives and the social responsibility which is tied to the growing knowledge base.

This concern with the future, technological change and ever-more complex social implications and responsibilities indicates the strong political and ethical dimensions of e-learning research—aspects of which have implications for whose learning will be enhanced and what the costs are, social, political and economic, of being "left behind". Despite its undoubted established status, however, researching e-learning in the "real world" (and probably because of it), was labelled "messy" by Seale (2003)—and it still is. This chapter explores this "messiness" and the ways in which recent research has made sense of it, to examine whether potentially coherent frameworks exist for conceptualizing e-learning research which can be relevant in such a diverse field.

Maturation of e-learning research

Conole (2003) has analysed developments in what she termed a developing and "eclectic" field with a "pattern of emergence" (p. 130) that is between the stages of "diversification" ("the area starts to mature and different schools of thought emerge") and "establishment" (it "becomes recognized in its own right ... perceived of as 'respected' research"). In 2003 she argued for the importance of identifying linking characteristics in this diverse field that reflect the political and contested nature of e-learning research and proposed them as (p. 131):

- interdisciplinarity and multiple voices
- change
- convergence and interoperability
- interactivity and social interaction
- politics.

These linking characteristics could be found within the three main research themes in the field which she argued to be: pedagogical, technical and operational. Conole (2003: 139) emphasized the importance of "the sense of shared ownership and co-participation in learning technology research, in part because of the practical pragmatic dimension to the area, but also because of the highly political nature and dependences on stakeholder perspectives".

It is interesting to see the development over time of this approach to understanding coherence and linkages in the field. Four years later Conole and Oliver (2007) increased this to six unifying themes and, in a significant move, added "access and inclusion" to the above. "Convergence and interoperability" became "commodification" in a more encompassing concern for research to address and contribute to an integrated perspective on technologies as embedded in wider social and educational concerns. Similarly, they identified the field as concerned not so much with distinct themes, but with e-learning contexts in which the linking concerns might interplay. They proposed that these contexts for research are now: the relation between e-learning and areas of policy formation and implementation, organizational structures and roles, learning theory, technologies for learning and the epistemological and methodological alternatives open to researchers. Such a move seeks to unify disparate research foci by concentrating on the social and ethical consequences of research, which challenges the ways in which "knowledge" is organized, developed and disseminated—"owned"—in contemporary contexts.

Moves towards unifying concepts of e-learning research shift away from both vertical (with a focus on "chronologies" or "eras" or research) and horizontal (focusing on "taxonomies" of research types and methodologies) ways of classifying e-learning research, which were an earlier way for researchers to orientate themselves in a still-new field and to attempt to interpret coherent patterns in its evolution. There is, of course, relevance in understanding "where we have been" in order to understand the inter-relationship between research and its contexts in the current ecology of e-learning.

E-learning research has been described as a "chameleon field" (Snyder, 1999: xxv) and, in relation to the impact of technologies on cognition, seeking to understand something which has remained persistently elusive (Laurillard, 2002; Rourke and Kanuka, 2007). Contexts for e-learning evolve rapidly as patterns of student participation change along with technological advances. A range of new contexts, such as distance education, mass education and work-based learning including a huge range of forms of vocational training and professional accreditation, make demands on research to provide insights into effective learning in new conditions in which people learn over the course of a lifetime. One emergent focus has been on the contribution of e-learning to work-based learning and professional development. Adult professional learning communities have been the subject of increasing investigation as more higher education institutions offer accreditation for work-based learning. Shih, Feng and Tsai (2008) found that there were two areas—meta-cognition among e-learners and the learning of adults outside of formal environments—which were under-represented in research into cognition and technology and ripe for further investigation considering the growth of interest in lifelong learning and the contribution of meta-cognition to learning over a lifetime.

At the same time as these developments, providers are constrained by unfavourable global economic conditions, with universities under increasing pressure to improve student retention and learning experiences at a time of cuts in expenditure and reduced investment in staff development. There has always been a danger of e-learning being seen as a cheap alternative to traditional teaching modes and the current climate may inevitably encourage a view of e-learning as a panacea for economic downturn and cuts in higher-education budgets rather than as a research-informed pedagogical development within the sector. E-learners face challenges of potential isolation and the dilution of experience while they are coping with serial change and multiple pressures in the workplace and with economic and social unease. E-learning research thus has a complex relationship with reality. Laurillard (2008b: 139–40) warns about the problem of technology-driven research:

> Education has problems. Technology has solutions looking for problems. The two should fit, and this conviction fuels the continuing interest in "technology enhanced learning". But the solutions technology brings, in their most immediate form, are solutions to problems education does not have.... It is a perfectly legitimate exercise to be inventive in our use of technological opportunities, but if we are always technology-led we get sub-optimal solutions. We might, for example, think up many uses for a sledgehammer—perhaps to crack nuts? It is imaginative and effective, but sub-optimal, because if you start with the problem of how best to crack a nut you develop a quite different tool. iPods were developed by working out the optimal technological solution for people who wanted to listen to music, not for people wanting

to learn. If we want to create the optimal technological solutions for the requirements of education, we need the equivalent of nutcrackers, not sledgehammers, to crack that nut.

Where the "two should fit" but do not, there is an ecological dilemma. Key elements in the ecology of e-learning (e.g. technological innovations) have disproportionate or inappropriate impact on others (e.g. technology adoption policy in education institutions), the results distorting the coherence of the environment as a whole. A different perspective on the ecology of e-learning research is needed, one in which mutuality can be established between research foci, technology and educational purpose. The relationship between e-learning research and the socio-cultural and educational context has always been problematic. A chronological perspective shows how early research focused on technocentric solutions to educational problems, within an "information age" perspective (Andriessen, Baker and Suthers 2003) which was, arguably, superseded by a "knowledge age" in which the focus shifted to the nature of the educational transaction between learners and the socio-technical resources available to them. Subsequent "second wave" research grew out of an increasing interest in the integration of technology into education contexts, in particular through "blended learning"—based on the concept of inherently different facets possessed by e-learning and "other" learning, which could be brought together in productive ways. This has been critiqued as persisting an unhelpful dichotomy between "types" of learning which has dominated research and development in formal education settings for over a decade (Oliver and Trigwell, 2005; Oliver, 2003).

Oliver (2003) has disputed the relevance of chronological accounts of e-learning research and development, such as the one proposed by Littlejohn and Peacock (2003: 78-84), who classified "eras" thus:

- the pioneering era (early 1990s)
- the practice era (mid-1990s)
- the policy era (Dearing 1997)[6]
- the pedagogy era (1999—e.g. "blended learning")
- the partnership era (2001—e.g. "portal era", linking communities).

Oliver's argument is that, in reality, "eras" co-exist and that people "may need to move up and down" the model over time "as new technologies emerge" (2003: 158). There are shortcomings, therefore, in a focus on the temporal dimensions of research, located in a history of ideas (important as they are) which established the new field. It is of course important to recognize that e-learning has a (disputed) history of ideas of its own. A different way of conceptualizing e-learning research is needed, however, one which is able to address the integration of temporal and contextual issues and be inclusive of the possibility of multiple distinct themes and also complex linkages between them. One such conceptualization is offered by Andrews (in Haythornthwaite et al., 2007) who proposes that a new way of conceptualizing e-learning research is needed which centres on the "co-evolution of technology and learning practices". He proposes that an appropriate research model can be both "for" and "about" e-learning. It is based on the argument that the relationship between ICT and learning is essentially reciprocal. Both new technologies and learning are bound together and develop together—they are "co-evolutionary":

> The relationship is not seen as causal or one-way as is conventionally the case, with assumptions that ICT has a causal impact on learning; rather, new technologies and learning are seen to develop alongside each other.

In Figure 6.1, the vertical axes represent what can be seen as the chronological perspective in which ICT and learning develop over time, each with its own characteristics but linked by a series of "horizontal" relationships between learning and ICT which are context-specific and "of the time". Andrews in Haythornthwaite et al. (2007) argues that there are also "residual" and "predictive" relationships between learning and ICT and that these have to be acknowledged within such a model, that can look at what has gone before and what is still being developed. The temporal and contextual dimensions of e-learning research are thus captured by such a model. It is possible to locate educational and technological questions at places along the axes, which helps to conceptualize where they contribute to and grow out of the wider concerns of the field—which can thus be seen as having an ecological coherence. A further aspect of this coherence is that Andrews in Haythornthwaite et al. (2007) claims that the model can be applied to different research epistemologies:

> It is useful for … studies about online learning and communities of practice, but can also be used for such research, as a tool for mapping the design of new e-learning resources and programs. For brevity's sake, I call this model a co-evolutionary model for e-learning research. For example, the development of wikis in Web

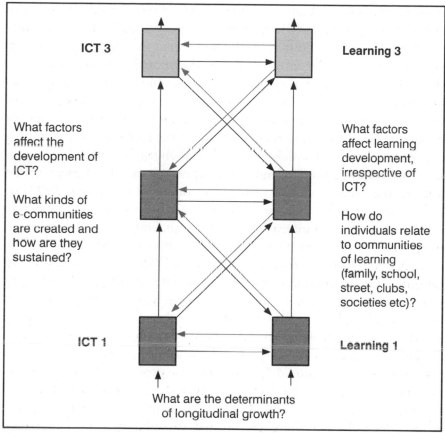

Figure 6.1   Co-evolutionary contextual model
Source: Andrews and Haythornthwaite, 2007: 40

2.0 technologies allows for an interactive and dialogic revision by a number of people of a text that might be lodged on a Web site. Further development of interactive technologies on the technologies side, and/or of learning practices in the co-editing of a common text on the learning side, might (most likely, will) create further possibilities in due course.

Researching the learning in e-learning

For educational researchers a persistent focus over time has been the transformational impact of technologies on cognition. This remains elusive and to understand this fully would support the much sought after "solution" to the challenge of harnessing technologies in the most effective ways. Laurillard warns against trying to describe "with completeness" (2002: 63) the learning process and has consistently warned (Laurillard 2008b: 139) that there is an "argument for starting with an understanding of the educational problems and using this analysis to target the solutions we should be demanding from technology". Too often in the past this has not been the case. Part of the problem is historical and lies within technology driven agendas for educational research, and related to this is the challenge of developing appropriate methods which are capable of engaging with e-learning as a highly complex human and social phenomenon. References in the field to the "sociocognitive turn" (Garrison and Anderson, 2003) or the "narrative turn" (Friesen, 2008) are indicative of sea-changes in epistemology and an increasing focus on qualitative paradigms which are capable of dealing with highly complex human practices.

Snyder stated that "critical borrowing" (1998: xxv) is necessary to develop e-learning research. By this she meant that researchers need not only to utilize the methods available from established disciplines such as the social sciences, semiotics and literary hermeneutics, but to adapt them and develop new ones in the light of new contexts for research and technologies available to support and construct it. Snyder suggests that research in this area should "grow out of the problems and questions in the field" (1998: xxv) and that creativity and adaptation is necessary to meet the new circumstances. "Growth" may involve bringing together fields which do not share established disciplinary processes which are deemed to cultivate and research knowledge. As it progresses, methodology will demand adaptation and creativity. This was a feature of "second wave" research into e-learning which evolved around the millennium which was characterized by the need to find appropriate methods to address the specificities of new learning practices within particular contexts. In particular, the development of "blended" learning called for a range of methods which could investigate learning across face to face and online contexts, most frequently based on computer-mediated communication (CMC).

Research in the area of cognitive change has increasingly utilized "mixed methods", drawing on quantitative and qualitative methods, as highlighted by Shih, Feng and Tsai (2008) in their review of the 16 most-frequently cited research articles from over four thousand studies conducted between 2001 and 2005, or "crossover methods" (Garrison and Anderson, 2003), referring to qualitative adaptation of quantitative approaches to textual analysis of online transcripts. Shih, Feng and Tsai (2008) emphasize that the commonalities between quantitative and qualitative research, as advocated by Johnson and Onwuegbuzie (2004), are appropriate for e-learning contexts, where there is a need for data which deals with participants' experiential and perceptual engagement with learning (e.g. by interviews and textual interpretation), as well as considerable quantities of data captured by the technologies themselves (e.g. online transcripts which can be subjected to electronic content analysis and records of participatory behaviours created by VLEs):

> Because online technology or databases in e-learning keep records of learners' learning processes, it allows researchers to make interpretations based on log files, discourse, or interaction records. It seems that the new study field of e-learning has brought researchers new methods of data collection. (Shih, Feng and Tsai, 2008).

Historically, the abundance of online data about learners' participatory behaviours within prevalent CMC e-learning contexts supported a mostly narrow range of quantitative approaches to analysing evidence of learning. The field includes a burgeoning literature on approaches to the analysis of online discussion and an array of taxonomies and methods categorizing features of the text to indicate that some form of learning is taking place. Research into CMC has had a positivist focus on counting or categorizing typified by: patterns of participant interaction (c.g. Salmon's (2004) nine "categories" for analysing discourse analysis into "individual" and "interactive" thinking); linguistic discourse features (e.g. Fahy's (2003) "Transcript Analysis Tool" which compares the frequencies and proportions of five sentence types—questions, statements, reflections, scaffolding/engaging, quotation/citation/paraphrase); language functions (e.g. Bradshaw, Chapman and Gee's (2002) "Evidence of Learning Taxonomy" based on learning actions within the text, e.g. offering ideas, asking, articulating, exploring). These studies used methods which are readily quantifiable and relatively easy to identify but offered little in-depth analysis of the complex psychological phenomenon of learning in a social-interactive context. Rovai (2003) and McGorry (2003) developed methods to gauge the impact of CMC on learning from a learner's perspective. McGorry's Likert scale, used to gauge students' experiences, collects data based on self-report. Using a numerical mean derived from Likert scales to indicate what is happening in the online forum is only a very reduced interpretation of the experience of learning however. Rovai categorizes evaluation "types" and focuses on "input", "process", "output" and "impact" to help structure an analysis of the student experience. "Process" is the tricky part of this, which is the only "type" to do with the actual learning that is happening and how it is happening, and offers little to work with in a practical or theoretical way. Both models are rooted in managerial/evaluation concerns rather than theory-building. Such research approaches are rooted in methods which, although claiming to show that learning is taking place within constructivist frameworks, offer little to show how methodologically there is a link between the methods used and the claims for evidence of knowledge construction which emerge.

The problem has been a lack of analytical tools that tell us about learning transformations in ways which address the complexities of the phenomenon. The chief methodological concern for investigating the prevalent e-learning mode over the past decade—CMC—was how to examine the transcripts of asynchronous, text-based discussions, thereby addressing Lapadat's (2000) methodological challenge: "Can conceptual change be identified and tracked?" More qualitative approaches were developed, focusing on levels of reflexivity and higher order thinking as well as the nature of participants' cognitive engagement and conceptual change. These have focused on identifying the capacities of participants to make reasoned decisions, adapt to change, reason critically, collaborate productively, work independently, see multiple perspectives, be able to solve problems and engage in negotiating meaning (see e.g. Lapadat, 2000; Laurillard et al., 2000; McLoughlin and Luca, 2000; Smith, 2003). Preece and Maloney-Krichmar (2005) have shown that where a contrasting qualitative approach was adopted, ethnography was a popular choice of many researchers to understand the social participatory aspects of communicating online, focusing on describing the social practices which people engage in and the community building aspects of these. A significant challenge in all these studies, however, has been the lack of transferability of indicators that capture the complexities of human learning in a way that makes them reliable across different contexts.

The "narrative turn"

Friesen (2008) has analysed the marginalization of narrative approaches to e-learning research and makes a case for its relevance to technology-rich educational settings. The claim is that "narrative interpenetrates and saturates e-learning practice and research" (p. 297), so great is the significance of narrative in the individual's construction of meaning in everyday life. His argument is that, as a research tool, narrative approaches to both data collection (e.g. by narrative interviewing) and analysis (by researcher interpretation) offer insights into complexity which are needed in order for us to *learn* rather than to *prove* (after Bruner, 1986; see also Pachler, Cook and Bradley, 2009). Narrative is one means by which, arguably, both the "situated" and the "generalizable" can be extracted from the data, as he demonstrates in his analysis of a case, "Lisa":

> The kind of knowledge or lessons that can be derived from this particular narrative for research and practice in e-learning are situated, practical, and in some ways, personal in nature. Lisa's story can be said to inform e-learning research by providing valuable knowledge about the use of computer and Internet technology in the case of her classroom and others like it. To use more logico-scientific language, Lisa's narrative suggests that the careful integration of blogs into a writing-intensive course can result in increased student participation, and also in new forms of student participation, such as peer comments on writing, and informal, extracurricular writing in the target language of instruction. (Friesen, 2008: 304)

Until recently (Conole et al., 2008; Creanor et al., 2006; Daly et al., 2007), the contribution of narrative methodology to research about e-learner experiences of learning has been neglected. The growth in narrative methods is based on the conviction, borrowed from research in the social sciences, that they have the flexibility that is necessary to capture and record the complexities of human experiential phenomena (Czarniaswska, 2004; Elliott, 2005). Narrative is a way of engaging qualitatively with experiential data, enabling understanding of learning experiences from the dual perspective of both the learner and the researcher. For the learner, constructing narratives is an act of sense-making by which experiences are organized and articulated in social contexts. The learners' narratives provide accounts in which they organize their experience of participating in particular ways, to make it meaningful to them and communicable and comprehensible to the researcher in dialogic contexts, including online forums, online commentaries and focus groups and interviews (Daly, 2008a). Participants' narratives of their learning have the potential to offer unique interpretations of it as a lived practice, both individual and social.

Friesen (2008) suggests there is a strong argument for rich research methods which reveal more than "logico-scientific" experimental approaches in which technology is introduced as an experimental intervention, usually based on a comparative study model:

> These studies have gained notoriety for the particular finding of "no significant difference" that they have produced through many and varied iterations. This final result is associated with what has come to be known as the "no significant difference phenomenon". This phrase, of course, refers to hundreds of media comparison studies that have attempted to measure student achievement and that report that the introduction of technology or media did *not* make a statistically significant difference in terms of this metric. (p. 306)

Researching cognition in e-learning

Shih, Feng and Tsai's (2008) content analysis of studies in e-learning found that "almost half (43.2%, 444 of 1027 articles) of the articles published in five educational journals from 2001 to 2005 were related to the field of cognition in e-learning". Questionnaires persisted as the main method of gathering data in the 16 most-cited articles, but there was a "clear trend" towards using online content and learners' logs as research data. This "trend" can be observed in the expansion in qualitative analysis approaches to analysing online communication between learners. They point out the limitations of questionnaire methods and growing interest in a wider range of qualitative approaches.

As a strategy which seeks to address the needs of qualitative researchers, the content analysis approach has been developed over time by a continuing refinement in qualitative adaptations of a content analysis model (Anderson and Kanuka, 2003; Anderson et al., 2001; Garrison and Anderson, 2003; Garrison, Anderson and Archer, 2001) to include a methodology outlined by Garrison and Anderson as an "inductive" application of content analysis to transcripts of online exchanges between learners.

> Qualitative content analysis [QCA] allows … for the emerging interpretation of the researcher to guide the analysis … allows us to position, relate, and ultimately understand the abstractly inferred content from higher-level processing of the text and interaction … thereby allows us to work with the meanings that underlie the content rather than directly with the content. (Anderson and Kanuka, 2003: 176)

In a series of research partnerships these researchers have grappled with the methodological problems of reconciling the fact that we do not read data "naively" in a situation where the researcher is close to the data and frequently has multiple investments in it, for example, as a contributory factor to course development. It is *how* to work with the knowledge, values and dispositions that researchers bring to the interpretation that is the source of their ongoing development of a model for Qualitative Content Analysis.

The Qualitative Content Analysis model

This model has been highly influential for a decade of e-learning research. Garrison and Anderson's approach to understanding intellectual progress in CMC is developed from what they identify as the constituent elements of a community of inquiry. Their concept of a "community of inquiry" is a methodological approach with high potential to be adapted across e-learning contexts to examine the qualitative aspects of participants' thinking which are necessary within an "inquiry" perspective (see Figure 4.3, Chapter 4). This is because a community of inquiry fosters critical thinking through "self-correcting practice driven by dialogue" within the community where "community evokes a sense of cooperation, trust and common purpose" (Parsell and Duke-Yonge, 2007: 182). Garrison and Anderson's model is based on the premise that a community of inquiry develops critical thinking through the interdependence of two critical processes—cognitive and social. Cognitive presence corresponds to phases of practical inquiry, beginning with a "triggering event" and involving "exploration" and "integration" of ideas, finally achieving "resolution". Social presence is key to critical thinking where it is constitutive of "open, affective communication and group cohesion" (Garrison and Anderson, 2003: 30). Garrison and Anderson also argue that teaching presence is the third key element in learning within a community of inquiry, because "there is an inherent need for an architect and facilitator to design, direct, and inform the transaction" (p. 29). Three key elements are, therefore, argued as essential to learning in CMC and as a core object of research: cognitive presence, social presence and teaching presence. They establish categories which constitute these elements. These are derived from the researchers' experience of working with and researching online texts and from their knowledge of relevant theoretical perspectives. Thus, they invoke real world experience as well as theoretical knowledge in developing categories by which to read and interpret the text. In this approach the development of a methodology has a highly iterative relationship with the data. A preliminary reading of the text establishes indicators that the category exists. The indicators are derived from the "surface" of the text and are explicit and recognizable. They are not brought to the text from the "outer" world, but are identified as existing within the text. From this they build the first stage in a framework for analysing the quality of learning in online discussion based on the three core elements in Table 4.3, Chapter 4.

The transcript of online discussion is then coded inductively to find all the examples of each indicator. All the instances thus identified are the *manifest variables*. This is clearly a broad kind of categorization by which they suggest all forms of learning in CMC can be examined within a community of inquiry perspective. Their use of *elements, categories* and *indicators* as a way of organizing understanding about learning through CMC is, of course, rooted in the construction of taxonomies. However, the potential of this "crossover" technique from quantitative approaches, rooted in computer-aided analysis, lies in it addressing the need for an iterative relationship between the researcher's conceptualization and the evidence as it emerges from the text, an interpretive process by which the structure for coding evolves. The definition of elements of learning needs to be clear, and is a qualitative process because it is the researcher who determines these, based on coherent values and experience, and who makes this defensible within relevant theoretical perspectives.

They identify "latent variables" as a means of conducting further investigation of meaning beneath the surface of the text. It is the latent variables within the messages which are especially relevant to examining learning and are more difficult to observe.

> Latent variables ... include important concepts such as evidence of creative or critical thinking ... [they] must be inferred from manifest content and this inferential procedure inevitably provides opportunities for inconsistencies and error on the one hand and insight and interpretation on the other. The nature of the latent variable influences the manner in which it is identified and described. (Anderson and Kanuka, 2003: 175)

The identification and analysis of latent variables has become a key methodological strategy in researching cognition in e-learning involving intuition and imagination in the interpretation of the data. In this approach the coding is based on a framework or typology which is "induced" and applied to the content. The final stage of Qualitative Content Analysis proposes "an association between the manifest behaviours and latent variables such as critical thinking, judgement, and initiative" (Anderson and Kanuka, 2003: 175). Hermeneutic understanding uses processes such as analogy and pattern recognition to draw conclusions about the meaning of linguistic messages.

Such an inductive methodology, which works explicitly with the researchers' self-aware engagement with the wider e-learning practice under investigation, has been the subject of intense interest and debate. There has been continued review of the "problem arena" of researching CMC (Valcke and Martens, 2006) based on methodological flaws in research instruments which affect reliability and validity and of whether "deep and meaningful" learning can be achieved in Community of Inquiry contexts (Rourke and Kanuka, 2007, 2009). Rourke and Kanuka argue that the content analysis approach to identifying three types of presence in a community of inquiry—social, cognitive and teaching—fails to work consistently across different contexts. The particular problem lies in identifying cognitive presence, because very few empirical studies exist which have explored forms of presence utilizing methods which go beyond self-report and which apply rigorous approaches to identifying deep learning. They argue that only a minority of online interactions between learners consists of "critical discourse, mutual critique, or argumentation" (2009: 43). It appears that each application of content analysis in a community of inquiry requires a customization of the research instrument and the need for careful derivation of the categories and indicators used for analysis, meaning that the projection of theory is highly contextualized (Daly, 2008b).

Where next?

Research is developing in new directions to understand how e-learning can be responsive to the complex needs and learning aims involved in personalization, simulation and increased choice about learning pathways followed over a lifetime. "Student-centered instruction" has been identified as a primary trend in education by the year 2020 (Shih, Feng and Tsai, 2008), and future research agendas need to include learner and teacher experiences and investigate forms of evaluation which are appropriate to new learning modes and altered relations with fellow-learners and teachers:

> How to maintain and enhance students' learning motivation and teachers' teaching motivation in this constantly changing educational environment will be an essential issue for future studies. In the future, educators may need to pay more attention to studying learners' and teachers' motivation in e-learning environments…. Because the students themselves will become the center of the whole learning process in future education. (Shih, Feng and Tsai, 2008: 965)

Such moves will inevitably raise further ethical dimensions in e-learning research. Already, we are familiar with ethical quandaries around the conflation of e-learners' identities with their online presence. It has been argued that, in CMC contexts, the electronic author cannot be confused with his or her textual output (Bassett and O'Riordan, 2002; Borland, 1991), and much of the literature on e-portfolios has focused on technical aspects rather than their conceptual significance in changing the way learning is generated and represented by individuals. For example, e-portfolios are usually framed as little more than electronic versions of paper portfolios, whose benefits consist primarily of easier storage and manipulation and there has been little research into the ways in which technologies impact on the formation and representation of identity through e-portfolios as well as the process of reflection (McAlpine, 2005). Yet the e-learning literature has extensively explored the way in which digital technology in education transforms how knowledge and identity are generated. For example, the use of blogs, tweeting, collaboratively produced wikis and hotlinks affect how meta-reflection on learning can be achieved, evidenced, shared and assessed (Pachler and Daly, 2009). Simulation and Second Life experiences provide further challenges for educators to understand the interplay between learner identities and cognition as something both individual and socially constructed. This gap has particular significance for understanding how technologies shape learner identity and how learning and self-reflection emerge within a community existing primarily in digital form. There appears to be an ever-increasing need to work "responsibly" (Bassett and O'Riordan, 2002) in e-learning research contexts and to review what is required to work with what Capurro and Pingel (2002) call an "ethics of care" and with "social responsibility" (Anderson and Kanuka, 2003).

Research into the affective and experiential aspects of e-learning was a late-comer to the field over the past decade. Oliver (2003: 156) argued for the need for research into "the motivational, affective aspect of the process that leads students into engagement [with learning]". In the following years, a range of research into the affective aspects of e-learning pedagogy and a focus on the learner experience came to the fore (e.g. Conole et al., 2008; Creanor et al., 2006; Daly et al., 2007) supported by initiatives such as the JISC "Understanding my Learning" project started in 2005. Such studies draw attention to the persistent and varied experiences of e-learners who are in transition between states and processes that have varying degrees of familiarity, both social and intellectual. The transitions are partly to do with adjusting to new ways of establishing social relations in new collaborative contexts and, related to this, to do with learning how to learn—what Levy (2006) has termed the "process" domain of learning with e-pedagogies, indicating that "what becomes vital in this scenario is a focus on developing the person's sensibilities to being an e-learner and evaluating the processes of change and adaptation in a way which supports him or her in the 'newness' of the practices of e-learning" (Daly et al., 2007: 458).

The theory–practice challenge for e-learning research

E-learning practice has proliferated across the education sectors and beyond over the past 20 years, but in many instances this has been arguably *regardless of* e-learning research rather than informed by it. There is an acknowledged gap between the growing research base and much policy-making in education institutions regarding adoption, course design and, crucially, practitioner development (Hadjithoma-Garstka 2009; Kezar, 2000; Mellar, Oliver and Hadjithoma-Garstka 2009). Laurillard (2008b) argues that teachers and lecturers "have too little help in addressing the issue at the heart of our educational problems: 'how to identify and provide what it takes to learn' " (p.140). The research culture of HE institutions, reward systems which focus on research rather than practice, and lack of time for developing and applying research findings to practice are all familiar issues which contribute to the problem.

A disciplinary focus has been argued as one way to link the two, for example, in language learning contexts which have an established history of distance education and interactional pedagogies as underpinning features of e-learning developments, leading the way in adoption of synchronous and asynchronous forums for language exchange, online writing and audiographic conferencing. Lamy and Hampel (2007) argue that for practitioners a discipline-focused approach based on "action research" and "exploratory practice" (which "puts understanding a situation above solving a problem" (p. 159)) ensures that the relationship between theory and practice is reciprocal, so that "practical applications of theoretical concepts can lead to an interrogation and modification of the original theory" (p. 105). Practitioner research is the goal here, but for many academics, engaging in this still requires additional infrastructure to support new areas and out-of-field research.

A large part of the challenge is how to harness the expertise which exists in pockets of innovative and research-informed practice within education institutions and instigate an e-learning research culture which is inclusive of practitioners from a range of disciplines. Mellar, Oliver and Hadjithoma-Garstka (2009) report the challenges and potentials of connecting e-learning research communities with practitioner colleagues within a university context in the Higher Education Academy Pathfinder project "From Pedagogic Research to Embedded E-Learning" (PREEL). Obstacles are identified in how research conducted by colleagues can be made immediately applicable to other specific contexts, no matter how related or similar they may appear to be:

> Researchers (even those who also teach) always found it a challenge to present research in such a way as to make it applicable. This arose from the stance they adopted as researchers, pursuing generalisable knowledge, in contrast with the practitioners' particular needs for applicable teaching guidance. Research was generally conceptualised as problematics rather than solutions or "how-to" formulae, so could be seen as addressing the researcher's concerns rather than the practitioner's. (p. 169)

This is of course not a new dilemma—the gap between "theory" and "practice" in pedagogical practice is one with which we are all too familiar. But, e-learning blurs the boundaries more than ever between the roles of "tutor", "researcher" and "evaluator" in professional knowledge-building processes. The relationship between teaching, evaluation and research is in need of fundamental review (Daly et al., 2007) if research is to make the necessary *difference* to e-learning experiences. A different conceptualization is needed—one which extends Conole's concept of "messiness"—so that practitioners and researchers have roles as co-constructors of the body of knowledge about e-learning. A "co-evolutionary" perspective on e-learning (after

Andrews and Haythornthwaite, 2007) extends here to the conception of researcher-practitioner roles. The shift in focus to the person (tutor, researcher, evaluator, learner) who must utilize a range of socio-technical resources demands new ways of drawing on existing disciplinary fields and forging of new identities for researchers as well as for the "subjects" of their research.

Notes

1   e.g. *Research in Learning Technology*, *Computers & Education*, *E-Learning and Digital Media* and *Journal of Asynchronous Learning Networks* (JALN).
2   See e.g. CAL (Computer Assisted Learning)—http://www.cal-conference.elsevier.com/; ALT-C (Association for Learning Technology)—http://www.alt.ac.uk/altc2010/ and Educa Berlin—http://www.online-educa.com/.
3   http://www.tlrp.org/tel/.
4   http://www.jisc.ac.uk/.
5   http://www.obhe.ac.uk/home.
6   https://bei.leeds.ac.uk/Partners/NCIHE/.

References

Allen, I. and Seaman, J. (2008) *Staying the course: Online education in the United States*. Needham, MA: Sloan Consortium.

Ambient Insight Research (2009) *US self-paced e-learning market*. Monroe, WA: Ambient Insight Research.

Anderson, T. (2008) "Towards a theory of online learning." In Anderson, T. (ed.) *The theory and practice of online learning*. 2nd edn. Edmonton, Canada: Athabasca University Press, pp. 45–68. Available at http://www.aupress.ca/books/120146/ ebook/99Z_Anderson_2008-Theory_and_Practice_of_Online_ Learning.pdf .

Anderson, T., and Kanuka, H. (2003) *E-research: Methods, strategies and issues*. Boston: Allyn and Bacon.

Anderson, T., Rourke, L., Garrison, D., and Archer, W. (2001) "Assessing teaching presence in a computer conferencing context." *Journal of Asynchronous Learning Networks* 5(2):2–17. Available at http://www.sloan-c.org/publications/ jaln/v5n2/v5n2_anderson.asp.

Andrews, R., and Haythornthwaite, C. (2007) (eds) *Handbook of e-learning research*. London: Sage.

Andriessen, J., Baker, M., and Suthers, D. (2003) "Argumentation, computer support, and the educational contexts of confronting cognitions." In Andriessen, J., Baker, M., and Suthers, D. (eds) *Arguing to learn: Confronting cognitions in computer-supported collaborative learning environments*. Dordrecht, The Netherlands: Kluwer Academic Publishers, pp. 1–25.

Angeli, C., and Valanides, N. (2008) "Epistemological and methodological issues for the conceptualization, development, and assessment of ICT–TPCK: Advances in technological pedagogical content knowledge (TPCK)." In *Computers & Education* 52 (1):154–68.

Attwell, G. (2005) *Recognising learning: Educational and pedagogical issues in e-portfolios*. Available at http://www.scribd.com/doc/24852254/Recognising-Learning-Educational-and-pedagogic-issues-in-e-Portfolios-Graham-Attwell.

Australian Flexible Learning Network (2004) *Assessment and online teaching*. Available at http://pre2005.flexiblelearning.net.au/guides/assessment.pdf.

Bachmair, B., Pachler, N., and Cook, J. (2009) "Mobile phones as cultural resources for learning: An analysis of educational structures, mobile expertise and emerging cultural practices." *MedienPädagogik*. Available at http://www.medienpaed.com.

Bakhtin, M. (1986) "The problems of speech genres." In Emerson, C., and Holquist, M. (eds) *Speech genres and other late essays*. Trans. V.W. McGee. Austin: University of Texas Press, pp. 60–101.

Banyard, P., Underwood, J., and Twiner, A. (2006) "Do enhanced communication technologies inhibit or facilitate self-regulated learning?" In *European Journal of Education* 41(3–4):473–89.

Baron, N. (2000) *Alphabet to email*. London: Routledge.

Barrett, H. (2004) *Electronic portfolios as digital stories of deep learning: Emerging digital tools to support reflection in learner-centred portfolios*. Available at http://electronicportfolios.com/digistory/epstory.html.

Bassett, E., and O'Rordan, K. (2002) "Ethics of internet research: Contesting the human subjects research model." *Ethics and Information Technology* 4(3):233–47. Available at http://www.nyu.edu/projects/nissenbaum/projects_ethics.html.

Beaudoin, M. (2008) "Book review." *The American Journal of Distance Education* 22:123–5.

Beck, U., Giddens, A., and Lash, S. (1994) *Reflexive modernization: Politics, tradition and aesthetics in the modern social order*. Cambridge: Polity.

Becta (2007) *Harnessing technology review 2007*. Coventry: Becta.

Becta (2008) *Harnessing technology review 2008*. Coventry: Becta.

Becta (2009) *Harnessing technology for next generation learning: Children, schools and families implementation plan 2009–2012*. Available at http://publications.becta.org.uk/display.cfm?resID=39547.

Becta (2010) *Harnessing technology review 2009: The role of technology in further education and skills*. Coventry: Becta.

BIS [Department for Business, Innovation and Skills] (2009) *Higher ambitions: The future of universities in a knowledge economy.* Belfast: The Stationery Office.

BIS and DCMS [Department for Business, Innovation and Skills and Department for Culture, Media and Sport] (2009) *Digital Britain: Final report.* London: The Stationery Office. Available at http://www.culture.gov.uk/images/publications/digitalbritain-finalreport-jun09.pdf.

Blake, N. (2000) "Tutors and students without faces or places." *Journal of Philosophy of Education* 34(1):183–96.

Black, P., and Wiliam, D. (1998) "Assessment and classroom learning." *Assessment in Education* 5(1):7–74.

Black, P., and Wiliam, D. (2009) "Developing the theory of formative assessment." *Educational Assessment, Evaluation and Accountability* 21(1):5–31.

Borgman, C., Abelson, H., Dirks, L, Johnson, R., Koedinger, K., Linn, M., Lynch, C., Oblinger, D., Pea, R., Salen, K., Smith, M., and Szalay, A. (2008) *Fostering learning in the networked world: The cyberlearning opportunity and challenge: A 21st century agenda for the National Science Foundation.* Report of the NSF Task Force on Cyberlearning. Available at http://www.nsf.gov/pubs/2008/nsf08204/nsf08204.pdf.

Borland, K. (1991) " 'That's not what I said': Interpretive conflict in oral narrative research." In Guck, S., and Patai, D. (eds) *Women's words: The feminist practice of oral history.* London: Routledge.

Bradshaw, P., Chapman, C. and Gee, A. (2002) *A report on the ULTRALAB's development of online components in NCSL programmes.* Chelmsford: Ultralab.

Bransford, J., Brown, A., and Cocking, R. (1999) *How people learn: Brain, mind experience and school.* Washington, DC: National Research Council. Available at http://www.nap.edu/html/howpeople1/.

Brown, J. (2002) "Know thyself: The impact of portfolio development on adult learning." *Adult Education Quarterly* 52(3):228–45.

Brown, J. and Adler, R. (2008) "Minds on fire: Open education, the long tail and learning 2.0." *EDUCAUSE Review* 43(1):16–32. Available at http://www.educause.edu/ir/library/pdf/ERM0811.pdf.

Bruner, J. (1985) "Narrative and paradigmatic modes of thought." In Eisner, E. (ed) *Learning and teaching the ways of knowing.* Chicago: University of Chicago Press, pp. 97–115.

Bruner, J. (1986) *Actual minds, possible worlds.* Cambridge, MA: Harvard University Press.

Butler, P. (2006) *A review of the literature on portfolios and electronic portfolios.* Massey University College of Education, Palmerston North. Available at https://eduforge. org/docman/view.php/142/1101/ePortfolio%20Project%20R esearch%20Report.pdf.

Capurro, R., and Pingel, C. (2002) "Ethical issues of online communication research". Paper presented at Computer Ethics: Philosophical Enquiries (CEPE) Conference, December 2001. Available at http://www.nyu.edu/projects/ nissenbaum/projects_ethics.html.

Clark, W., and Neumann, T. (2009) *Eportfolios: Models and implementation.* WLE Centre occasional paper in work-based learning 5. London: WLE Centre, Institute of Education. Available at http://www.wlecentre.ac.uk/cms/ files/occasionalpapers/op5_eportfolios_models_and_ implementation.pdf.

Cole, M. (1996) *Cultural psychology: A once and future discipline.* Cambridge, MA: Belknap Press of Harvard University Press.

Conole, G. (2003) "Understanding enthusiasm and implementation: E-learning research questions and methodological issues." In Seale, J. (ed.) *Learning technology in transition.* Lisse: Swets & Zeitlinger, pp. 129–46.

Conole, G., de Laat, M., Dillon, T., and Darby, J. (2008) "'Disruptive technologies', 'pedagogical innovation': What's new? Findings from an in-depth study of students' use and perception of technology." *Computers & Education* 50(2):511–24.

Conole, G., and Fill, K. (2005) "A learning design toolkit to create pedagogically effective learning activities." *Journal of Interactive Media in Education.* Available at http://www-jime.open.ac.uk/2005/08/conole-2005-08.pdf.

Conole, G., and Oliver, M. (2002) "Embedding theory into learning technology practice with toolkits." *Journal of Interactive Media in Education.* Available at: http://www-jime.open. ac.uk/2002/8/conole-oliver-02-8.pdf.

Conole, G., and Oliver, M. (2007) *Contemporary perspectives in e-learning research.* New York: Routledge, 2007.

Conole G., Oliver M., Dyke M., and Seale J. (2004) "Mapping pedagogy and tools for effective learning design." *Computers & Education* 43(1–2):17–33.

Convery, A. (2009) "The pedagogy of the impressed: How teachers become victims of technological vision." *Teachers and Teaching: Theory and Practice* 15(1):25–41.

Cox, M., Webb, M., Abbott, C., Blakeley, B., Beauchamp, T., and Rhodes, V. (2003) *ICT and pedagogy: A review of the research literature.* London: Becta for the Department for Education and Skills.

Creanor, L., Trinder, K., Gowan, D., and Howells, C. (2006) *LEX: The learner experience of e-learning: Final project report.* Available at http://www.jisc.ac.uk/uploaded_documents/ LEX%20Final%20Report_August06.pdf.

Cuban, L. (2001) *Oversold and underused: Computers in the classroom.* Cambridge, MA: Harvard University Press.

Czarniaswka, B. (2004) *Narratives in social science research.* London: Sage.

Daly, C. (2008a) "Evaluation for new learning contexts: How can it be 'fit for purpose'?" *Reflecting Education* 4 (1):127–38. Available at http://www.reflectingeducation.net.

Daly, C. (2008b) "The impact of text-based computer-mediated communication on teachers' professional learning." PhD thesis. Institute of Education, London.

Daly, C., and Pachler, N. (2007) "Learning with others in mind". In Pickering, J., Daly, C., and Pachler, N. (eds) *New designs for teachers' professional learning.* Bedford Way papers. London: Institute of Education, University of London, pp. 51–86.

Daly, C., and Pachler, N. (2010) "E-learning: The future?" In Arthur, J., and Davies, I. (eds) *Routledge textbook on educational studies.* London: Routledge, pp. 216–26.

Daly, C., Pachler, N., and Lambert, D. (2004) "Teacher learning: Towards a professional academy." *Teaching in Higher Education* 9(1):99–111.

Daly, C., Pachler, N., and Pelletier, C. (2009a) *ICT CPD for school teachers: A literature review for Becta.* Coventry: Becta. Available at http://partners.becta.org.uk/index. php?section=rh&catcode=_re_rp_02&rid=17359.

Daly, C., Pachler, N., and Pelletier, C. (2009b) *Continuing professional development in information and communications technology for teachers.* Coventry: Becta. Available at http://research. becta.org.uk/upload-dir/downloads/ict_cpd_report2.pdf.

Daly, C., Pachler, N., and Pickering, J. (2003) "Teacher learning and computer-mediated communication." *International Journal of Learning* 10:2897–2907.

Daly, C; Pachler, N.; Pickering, J., and Bezemer, J. (2007) "Teachers as e-learners: Exploring the experiences of teachers in an online professional masters programme." *Journal of In-service Education* 33(4):443–61.

Darling, L. (2001) "Portfolio as practice: The narratives of emerging teachers." *Teaching and Teacher Education* 17(1):107–21.

Davis, N. (2008) "How may teacher learning be promoted for educational renewal with IT? Models and theories of IT diffusion." In Voogt, J., and Knezek, G. (eds) *International handbook of information technology in primary and secondary education.* New York: Springer, pp. 507–40.

Dede, C. (2006) *Online professional development for teachers.* Cambridge, MA: Harvard University Press.

de Freitas, S., Oliver, M., Mee, A., and Mayers, T. (2007) "The practitioner perspective on the modeling of pedagogy and practice." *Journal of Computer Assisted Learning* 24(1):26–38.

Derry, J. (2007) "Epistemology and conceptual resources for the development of learning technologies." *Journal of Computer Assisted Learning* 23(6):503–10.

de Waale, R. (2010) "Mobile trends 2020." Available at http://www.m-trends.org/2010/01/mobile-trends-2020.html.

Dewey, J. (1938) *Experience and education.* New York: Collier Macmillan.

DfES [Department for Education and Skills] (2003) *Towards an e-learning strategy.* London: HMSO.

DfES [Department for Education and Skills] (2005) *Harnessing technology: Transforming learning and children's services.* Available at http://publications.dcsf.gov.uk//DownloadHandler.aspx?ProductId=DFES-1296-2005&VariantID=Harnessing+technology&.

Dourish, P. (2004) "What we talk about when we talk about context." *Personal and Ubiquitous Computing* 8(1):19–30.

Doyle, W., and Carter K. (2003) "Narrative and learning to teach: Implications for teacher-education curriculum." *Journal of Curriculum Studies* 35:129–37.

Elliott, J. (2005) *Using narrative in social research: Qualitative and quantitative approaches.* London: Sage.

Empirica (2006) *Benchmarking access and use of ICT in European schools 2006.* Bonn: Empirica.

ESRC [Economic and Social Research Council] (2008a) *Theorising the benefits of new technology for youth: Controversies of learning and development*. The educational and social impact of new technologies on young people in Britain 1. Oxford: University of Oxford.

ESRC [Economic and Social Research Council] (2008b) *Changing spaces: Young people, technology and learning.* The educational and social impact of new technologies on young people in Britain 2. Oxford: University of Oxford.

European Commission (2008) *The use of ICT to support innovation and lifelong learning for all.* Report on the Education and Training 2010 Work Programme. Brussels: European Commission.

Fahy, P. (2003) "Indicators of support in online interaction." *International Review of Research in Open and Distance Learning* 4(1). Available at http://www.irrodl.org/content/v4.1/fahy.html.

Fayard, A-L., and DeSanctis, G. (2005) "Evolution of an online forum for knowledge management professionals: A language game analysis." *Journal of Computer-Mediated Communication* 10(4). Available at http://jcmc.indiana.edu/vol10/issue4/fayard.html

Finnegan, R. (2003) "Meaning and learning". Keynote lecture at the Learning Conference on What Learning Means, Institute of Education University of London, June.

Fisher, T., Higgins, C., and Loveless, A. (2006) *Teachers learning with digital technologies: A review of research and projects.* Futurelab Series 14. Available at http://www.futurelab.org.uk/research/lit_reviews.htm#lr14.

Franklin, T., and Van Harmelen, M. (2007) *Web 2.0 for learning and teaching in higher education.* London: The Observatory of Borderless Higher Education. Available at http://www.obhe.ac.uk/resources-new/pdf/651.Pdf.

Friesen, N. (2008) "Chronicles of change: The narrative turn and e-learning research." *E-learning* 5(3):297–309.

Garrison, R., and Anderson, T. (2003) *E-learning in the 21st century: A framework for research and practice.* London: Routledge.

Garrison, R., Anderson, T., and Archer, W. (2000) "Critical inquiry in a text-based environment: Computer conferencing in higher education." *The Internet and Higher Education* 2(2–3):87–105. Available at http://communitiesofinquiry.com/files/Critical_Inquiry_model.pdf.

Garrison, D., Anderson, T., and Archer, W. (2001) "Critical thinking, cognitive presence and computer conferencing in distance education." *American Journal of Distance Education* 15(1):7–23. Available at http://www.atl.ualberta.ca/cmc/ CTinTextEnvFinal.pdf.

Garrison, R., and Kanuka, H. (2004) "Blended learning: Uncovering its transformative potential in higher education." *The Internet and Higher Education* 7(2):95–105.

Giddens, A. (1994) *Beyond left and right: The future of radical politics*. Cambridge: Polity.

Godwin-Jones, R. (2005) "Messaging, gaming, peer-to-peer sharing: Language learning strategies and tools for the millennial generation." *Language Learning and Technology* 9(1):17–22. Available at http://llt.msu.edu/vol9num1/emerging/default. html.

Goodyear, P. (2009) "Foreword." In Dirckinck-Holmfeld, L., Jones, C., and Lindström, B. (eds) *Analysing networked learning practices in higher education and continuing professional development*. Rotterdam: Sense Publisher, pp. vii–x.

Goodyear, P., Banks, S., Hodgson, V., and McConnell, D. (2004) *Advances in research on networked learning*. Kluwer: Dordrecht.

Hadjithoma-Garstka, C. (2009) "The gap between (e-learning) research and practice in higher education: Discussion from a theoretical perspective." *Journal of Higher Education*.

Haller, M. (2008) "Interactive displays and next-generation interfaces." *Emerging Technologies for Learning* 3:91–101. Available at http://partners.becta.org.uk/upload-dir/downloads/ page_documents/research/emerging_technologies08_chapter6. pdf.

Hammond, M., Crosson, S., Fragkouli, E., Ingram, J., Johnston-Wilder, P., Johnston-Wilder, S., Kingston, Y., Pope, M., and Wray, D. (2009) "Why do some student teachers make very good use of ICT? An exploratory case study." *Technology, Pedagogy and Education* 18(1):59–73.

Harasim, L. (2000) "Shift happens: Online education as a new paradigm in learning." *The Internet and Higher Education* 3(1–2):41–61.

Hardy, I. (2008) "The impact of policy upon practice: An Australian study of teachers' professional development." *Teacher Development* 12(2):103–13.

Hauge, T. (2006) "Portfolios and ICT as means of professional learning in teacher education." *Studies in Educational Evaluation* 32(1):23–36.

Haythornthwaite, C., Bruce, B., Andrews, R., Kazmer, M., Montague, R-A., and Preston, C. (2007) "Theories and models of and for online learning." *First Monday* 12(8). Available at http://firstmonday.org/issues/issue12_8/haythorn/index.html.

HEFCE [Higher Education Funding Council for England] (2009) *Enhancing learning and teaching through the use of technology: A revised approach to HEFCE's strategy for e-learning.* Available at http://www.hefce.ac.uk/Pubs/hefce/2009/09_12/.

HEFCE and JISC [Higher Education Funding Council for England and Joint Information Systems Committee] (2005) *HEFCE strategy for e-learning.* 2005/12. London: Higher Education Funding Council for England.

Hewitt, J., and Scardamelia, M. (1998) "Design principles for distributed knowledge building processes." *Educational Psychology Review* 10(1):75–96.

Hill, J. (1996) "Psychological sense of community: Suggestions for future research." *Journal of Community Psychology* 25(4):431–8.

Honey, P., and Mumford, A. (1986) *The manual of learning styles.* Maidenhead: P. Honey.

Hrastinski, S. (2008) "What is online learner participation: A literature review." *Computers & Education* 51(4):1755–65.

Hrastinski, S. (2009) "A theory of online learning as online participation." *Computers & Education* 52(1):78–82.

Hughes, G. (2009) "Social software: New opportunities for challenging social inequalities in learning?" *Learning, Media and Technology* 34(4):291–305.

Hutchings, P., and Shulman, L. (1999) "The scholarship of teaching: New elaborations, new developments." *Change* 31(5):10–15. Available at http://www.carnegiefoundation.org/elibrary/scholarship-teaching-new-elaborations-new-developments.

Hymes, D. (1994) "Towards ethnographies of communication." In Maybin, J. (ed.) *Language and literacy in social practice.* Clevedon: Multilingual Matters/Open University.

Ito, M., Horst, H., Bittanti, M., Boyd, D., Herr-Stephenson, B., Lange, P., Pascoe, C., and Robinson, L. *Living and learning with new media: Summary of findings from the digital youth project (2008).* The John D. and Catherine T. MacArthur Foundation Reports on Digital Media and Learning, Chicago: The MacArthur Foundation. Available at http://digitalyouth.ischool.berkeley.edu/report.

Jara, M., and Mellar, H. (2010) "Quality enhancement for e-learning courses: The role of student feedback." *Computers & Education* 54(3):709–14.

Jara, M., and Mohamad, F. (2007) *Pedagogical templates for e-learning*. WLE Centre occasional paper in work-based learning 2. WLE Centre, Institute of Education: London. Available at http://www.wlecentre.ac.uk/cms/files/occasionalpapers/wle_op2.pdf.

Jimoyiannisa, A., and Komis, V. (2007) "Examining teachers' beliefs about ICT in education: Implications of a teacher preparation programme." *Teacher Development* 11(2):149–73.

JISC [Joint Information Systems Committee] (2004) *Effective practice with e-learning: A good practice guide in designing for learning*. Available at http://www.jisc.ac.uk/media/documents/publications/effectivepracticeelearning.pdf.

JISC [Joint Information Systems Committee] (2007) *In their own words: Exploring the learner's perspective on e-learning*. Available at http://www.jisc.ac.uk/media/documents/programmes/elearningpedagogy/iowfinal.pdf.

JISC [Joint Information Systems Committee] (2008a) *Effective practice with e-portfolios*. Available at http://www.jisc.org.uk/media/documents/publications/effectivepracticeeportfolios.pdf.

JISC [Joint Information Systems Committee] (2008b) *Exploring tangible benefits of e-learning: Does investment yield interest?* Northumbria University. Available at: http://www.jiscinfonet.ac.uk/publications/camel-tangible-benefits.pdf.

JISC [Joint Information Systems Committee] (2009) *Effective practice in a digital age: A guide to technology-enhanced learning and teaching*. Available at http://www.jisc.ac.uk/media/documents/publications/effectivepracticedigitalage.pdf.

Johnson, L., Levine, A., and Smith, R. (2008) *The 2008 Horizon Report*. Austin, TX: The New Media Consortium.

Johnson, L., Levine, A., and Smith, R. (2009) *The 2009 Horizon Report*. Austin, TX: The New Media Consortium.

Johnson, L., Levine, A., Smith, R., and Stone, S. (2010) *The 2010 Horizon Report*. Austin, Texas: The New Media Consortium. Available at http://www.nmc.org/pdf/2010-Horizon-Report.pdf.

Johnson, R., and Onwuegbuzie, A. (2004) "Mixed methods research: A research paradigm whose time has come." *Educational Researcher* 33(7):14–26.

Jonassen, D., and Land, S. (2000) "Preface". In Jonassen, D. and Land, M. (eds) *Theoretical foundations of learning environments*. Hillsdale, NJ: Lawrence Erlbaum, pp. 3–9.

Jones, C., and Dirckinck-Holmfeld, L. (2009) "Analysing networked learning practices." In Dirckinck-Holmfeld, L., Jones, C., and Lindström, B. (eds) *Analysing networked learning practices in higher education and continuing professional development*. Rotterdam: Sense Publisher, pp. 1–27,

Jones, C., Ferreday, D., and Hodgson, V. (2008) "Networked learning a relational approach: Weak and strong ties." *Journal of Computer Assisted Learning* 24(2):90–102.

Jones, R. (2002) "The problem of context in computer mediated communication". Paper presented at the Georgetown Roundtable on Language and Linguistics, 7–9 March. Available at http://personal.cityu.edu.hk/~enrodney/Research/ContextCMC.doc.

Kalantzis, M., and Cope, B. (2004) "Designs for learning." *E-learning* 1(1):38–93.

Kanuka, H., and Rourke, L. (2008) "Exploring amplifications and reductions associated with e-learning: Conversations with leaders of e-learning programs." *Technology, Pedagogy and Education* 17(1):5–15.

Kerres, M., and de Witt, C. (2003) "A didactical framework for the design of blended learning arrangements." *Journal of Educational Media* 28(2–3):101–13.

Kezar, A. (2000) "Understanding the research-to-practice gap: A national study of researchers' and practitioners' perspectives." In Kezar, A., and Eckel, P. (eds) *Moving beyond the gap between research and practice in higher education*. San Francisco: Jossey Bass, pp. 9–19.

Kirkwood, A. (2009) "E-learning: You don't always get what you hope for." *Technology, Pedagogy and Education* 18(2):107–21.

Koehler, M., and Mishra, P. (2005) "Teachers learning technology by design." *Journal of Computing in Teacher Education* 21(3):94–102.

Kolb, D. (2000) "Learning places: Building dwelling thinking online." *Journal of Philosophy of Education* 34(1):121–33.

Kollar, I., Fischer, F., and Hesse, F. (2006) "Collaboration scripts: A conceptual analysis." *Educational Psychology Review* 18(2):159–85.

Koschmann, T. (2003) "CSCL, argumentation, and Deweyan inquiry: Argumentation is learning." In Andriessen, J., Baker, M., and Suthers, D. (eds) *Arguing to learn: Confronting cognitions in computer-supported collaborative learning environments.* Dordrecht: Kluwer Academic Publishers.

Krämer, B., and Schmidt, H.-W. (2001) "Components and tools for on-line education." *European Journal of Education* 36(2):195–222.

Kress, G. (2000) "Design and transformation: New theories of meaning." In Cope, B., and Kalantis, M. (eds) *Multiliteracies: Literacy learning and the design of social futures.* London: Routledge, pp.153–61.

Kress, G. (2003) *Literacy in the new media age.* London: Routledge.

Kress, G., and Pachler, N. (2007) "Thinking about the 'm-' in mobile learning." In Pachler, N. (ed.) *Mobile learning: Towards a research agenda.* WLE Centre occasional papers in work-based learning 1. London: WLE Centre, Institute of Education, pp. 7–31. Available at http://www.wlecentre.ac.uk/cms/files/occasionalpapers/mobilelearning_pachler_2007.pdf.

Lamy, M-N., and Hampel, R. (2007) *Online communication in language teaching.* Basingstoke: Palgrave MacMillan.

Lapadat, J. (2000) "Tracking conceptual change: An indicator of online learning." Paper presented at the International Online Conference on Teaching Online in Higher Education. Available at http://as1.ipfw.edu/2000tohe/papers/lapadat.htm.

Lapadat, J. (2002) "Written interaction: A key component in online learning." *Journal of Computer Mediated Communication* 7(4). Available at http://jcmc.indiana.edu/vol7/issue4/lapadat. html.

Laurillard, D. (2002) *Rethinking university teaching: A conversational framework for the effective use of learning technologies.* 2nd edn. London: Routledge.

Laurillard, D. (2007) "Pedagogical forms of mobile learning: Framing research questions." In Pachler, N. (ed.) *Mobile learning: Towards a research agenda.* WLE Centre occasional papers in work-based learning 1. London: WLE Centre, Institute of Education, pp. 153–75. Available at http://www.wlecentre. ac.uk/cms/files/occasionalpapers/mobilelearning_pachler_2007. pdf.

Laurillard, D. (2008a) "Technology enhanced learning as a tool for pedagogical innovation." *Journal of Philosophy of Education* 42(3–4):521–33.

Laurillard, D. (2008b) "The teacher as action researcher: Using technology to capture pedagogic form." *Studies in Higher Education* 3 (2):139–54.

Laurillard, D., and Masterman, E. (2010) "Online collaborative TPD for learning design." In Lindberg, O., and Olofsson, A. (2009) *Online learning communities and teacher professional development: Methods for improved education delivery.* Hershey, PA: Information Science Reference, pp. 230–46.

Laurillard, D., Stratfold, M., Luckin, R., Plowman, L., and Taylor, J. (2000) "Affordances for learning in a non-linear narrative medium." *Journal of Interactive Media in Education* 2. Available at http://www-jime.open.ac.uk/00/2.

Lave, J., and Wenger, E. (1991) *Situated learning: Legitimate peripheral participation.* Cambridge: Cambridge University Press.

Levy, P. (2006) " 'Living' theory: A pedagogical framework for process support in networked learning." *Association for Learning Technology Journal* 14(3):225–40.

Littlejohn, A., and Peacock, S. (2003) "From pioneers to partners: The changing voices of staff developers." In Seale, J. (ed.) *Learning technology in transition.* Lisse: Swets & Zeitlinger, pp. 77–90.

Luckin, R. (2006) "Understanding learning contexts as ecologies of resources: From the zone of proximal development to learner generated contexts." In Reeves, T., and Yamashita, S. (eds) *Proceedings of World Conference on E-Learning in Corporate, Government, Healthcare, and Higher Education 2006.* Chesapeake, VA: AACE, pp. 2195–2202.

Luckin, R. (2007) "The learner centric ecology of resources: A framework for using technology to scaffold learning." *Computers & Education* 50(2):449–62.

Lunsford, R. (1997) "When less is more: Principles for responding in the disciplines." In Sorcinelli, M., and Elbow, P. (eds) *Writing to learn: Strategies for assigning and responding to writing across the disciplines.* San Francisco: Jossey-Bass.

Mayes, T., and de Freitas, S. (2004) *Review of e-learning theories, frameworks and models.* Bristol: JISC. Available at http://www.jisc.ac.uk/uploaded_documents/Stage%202%20Learning%20Models%20(Version%201).

Mayes, T., and de Freitas, S. (2007) "Learning and e-learning: The role of theory". In Beetham, H., and Sharpe, R. (eds) *Rethinking pedagogy in the digital age.* Abingdon and London: Routledge, pp. 13–15.

McAlpine, M. (2005) "E-portfolios and digital identity: Some issues for discussion." *E-learning* 2(4):378–87.

McCombs, B., and Vakili, D. (2005) "A learner-centred framework for e-learning." *Teachers College Record* 107(8):1582–1600.

McGorry, S. (2003) "Measuring quality in online programs." *The Internet and Higher Education* 6(2):159–77.

McLoughlin, C., and Luca, J. (2000) "Cognitive engagement and higher order thinking through computer conferencing: We know why but do we know how?" In Herrmann, A., and Kulski, M. (eds) *Flexible futures in tertiary teaching*. Proceedings of the 9th Annual Teaching Learning Forum, 2–4 February. Perth, WA: Curtin University of Technology. Available at http://lsn.curtin.edu.au/tlf/tlf2000/mcloughlin. html.

Means, B., Toyama, Y., Murphy, R., Bakia, M., and Jones, K. (2009) *Evaluation of evidence-based practices in online learning: A meta-analysis and review of online learning studies*. Washington, DC: US Department of Education. Available at http://www.ed.gov/rschstat/eval/tech/evidence-based-practices/finalreport.pdf.

Mellar, H., Oliver, M., and Hadjithoma-Garstka, C. (2009) "The role of research in institutional transformation." In Mayes, T., Morrison, D., Mellar, H., Bullen, P., and Oliver, M. (eds) *Transforming higher education through technology-enhanced learning*. York: The Higher Education Academy. Available at https://www. heacademy.ac.uk/assets/York/documents/ourwork/ learningandtech/Transforming-12.pdf.

Mercer, N. (1995) *The guided construction of knowledge*. Clevedon: Multilingual Matters.

Mishra , P., and Koehler, M. (2006) "Technological pedagogical content knowledge: A framework for teacher knowledge." *Teachers College Record* 108(6):1017–54.

Moss, G., Jewitt, C., Levacic, R., Armstrong, V., Cardini, A., and Castle, F. (2007) *The interactive whiteboards, pedagogy and pupil performance evaluation: An evaluation of the Schools Whiteboard Expansion (SWE) project: London Challenge*. Nottingham: DfES. Available at http://www.dfes.gov.uk/ research/data/uploadfiles/RR816.pdf.

Muilenburg, L., and Berge, Z. (2005) "Student barriers to online learning: A factor analytic study." *Distance Education* 26(1):29–48.

Nicol, D. (2007) "Principles of good assessment and feedback: Theory and practice." Keynote paper at Assessment Design for Learning Responsibility, 29–31 May. Available at http://www.reap.ac.uk/public/Papers/Principles_of_good_assessment_and_feedback.pdf.

Nicol, D., and Macfarlane-Dick, D. (2006) "Formative assessment and self-regulated learning: A model and seven principles of good feedback practice." *Studies in Higher Education* 31(2):199–218.

Nicol, D., and Milligan, C. (2006), "Rethinking technology-supported assessment in terms of the seven principles of good feedback practice." In Bryan, C. and Clegg, K. (eds) *Innovative Assessment in Higher Education*. London: Routledge. Available at http://tltt.strath.ac.uk/REAP/public/Resources/Nicol_Milligan_150905.pdf.

Nichols, M. (2003) "A theory for eLearning." *Educational Technology & Society* 6(2):1–10. Available at http://projects.edte.utwente.nl/pi/papers/LearningTheory.html.

O'Dowd, R., and Waire, P. (2009) "Critical issues in telecollaborative task design." *Computer Assisted Language Learning* 22(2):173–88.

Ofcom (2008) *Media literacy audit: Report on UK children's media literacy.* Available at http://stakeholders.ofcom.org.uk/binaries/research/media-literacy/ml_childrens08.pdf.

Oliver, M. (2003) "Looking backwards, looking forwards: An overview, some conclusions and an agenda." In Seale, J. (ed.) *Learning technology in transition*. Lisse: Swets & Zeitlinger, pp. 147–60.

Oliver, M. (2005) "The problem with affordance." *E-learning* 2(4):402–13.

Oliver, M., and Trigwell, K. (2005) "Can 'blended learning' be redeemed?" *E-learning* 2(1):17–26.

Pachler, N. (2007) (ed.) *Mobile learning: Towards a research agenda.* WLE Centre occasional paper in work-based learning 1. London: WLE Centre, Institute of Education. Available at http://www.wlecentre.ac.uk/cms/files/occasionalpapers/mobilelearning_pachler_2007.pdf.

Pachler, N. (2010) "The socio-cultural ecological approach to mobile learning: An overview." In Bachmair, B. (ed.) *Medienbildung in neuen Kulturräumen: Die deutschsprachige und britische Diskussion*. Wiesbaden: VS Verlag für Sozialwissenschaften, pp. 153–67.

Pachler, N., Bachmair, B., and Cook, J. (2010) *Mobile learning: Structures, agency, practice.* New York: Springer.

Pachler, N., Cook, J., and Bradley, C. (2009) " 'I don't really see it': Whither case-based approaches to understanding off-site and on-campus mobile learning?" In Vavoula, G., Pachler, N., and Kukulska-Hulme, A. (eds) *Researching mobile learning: Frameworks, tools and research designs.* Oxford: Peter Lang Publishing, pp. 77–95.

Pachler, N., and Daly, C. (2009) "Narrative and learning with Web 2.0 technologies: Towards a research agenda." *Journal of Computer Assisted Learning* 25(1):6–18.

Pachler, N., and Daly, C. (2006a) "Online communities and professional teacher learning: Affordances and challenges." In Sorensen, E., and Murchú, D. (eds) *Enhancing learning through technology.* Hershey, PA: Idea Group, pp. 1–28.

Pachler, N., and Daly, C. (2006b) "Professional teacher learning in virtual environments: Myth or reality." *E-learning* 3(1):63–75.

Pachler, N., Daly, C., and Lambert, D. (2003) "Teacher learning: Reconceptualising the relationship between theory and practical teaching in Masters level course development." In Günther, J. (ed.) *Quality assurance in distance-learning and e-learning.* Krems, Austria: European Association of Telematic Applications, pp. 7–25.

Pachler, N., Daly, C., Mor, Y., and Mellar, H. (2010) "Formative e-assessment: Practitioner cases." *Computers & Education* 54(3):715–21.

Pachler, N., Mellar, H., Daly, C. Mor, Y., Wiliam, D. (2009) *Scoping a vision for formative e-assessment: A project report for JISC.* London: WLE Centre/London Knowledge Lab. Available at http://www.jisc.ac.uk/media/documents/projects/scopingfinalreport.pdf.

Pachler, N., Pimmer, C., and Seipold, J. (2010) (eds) *Work-based mobile learning: Concepts and cases: A handbook for academics and practitioners.* Oxford: Peter Lang.

Parsell, M., and Duke-Yonge, J. (2007) "Virtual communities of enquiry: An argument for their necessity and advice for their creation." *E-learning* 4(2):181–93.

Pearson, M., and Naylor, S. (2006) "Changing contexts: Teacher professional development and ICT pedagogy." *Education and information technologies* 11:283–91.

Perry, W. (1970). *Forms of intellectual and ethical development in the college years: A scheme.* New York: Holt, Rinehart and Winston.

Pickering, J., Daly, C., and Pachler, N. (2007) (eds) *New designs for teachers' professional learning.* Bedford Way papers. London: Institute of Education, University of London.

Preece, J., and Maloney-Krichmar, D. (2005) "Online communities: Design, theory, and practice." *Journal of computer-mediated communication* 10(4). Available at http://jcmc.indiana.edu/vol10/issue4/preece.html.

Preston, C. (2004) *Learning to use ICT in classrooms: teachers' and trainees' perspectives: An evaluation of the English NOF ICT teacher training programme 1999–2003.* London: MirandaNet and the Teacher Training Agency.

Punie, Y. (2007) "Learning spaces: An ICT-enabled model of future learning in the knowledge-based society." *European Journal of Education* 42(2):185–99.

Ravenscroft, A. (2001) "Designing e-learning interactions in the 21st century: Revisiting and rethinking the role of theory." *European Journal of Education* 36(2):133–56.

Rheingold, H. (1991) *Virtual reality.* New York: Summit Books

Rose. J. (2008) *The independent review of the primary curriculum: Interim report.* Available at http://publications.teachernet.gov.uk.

Rourke, L., and Kanuka, H. (2007) "Barriers to online critical discourse." *Computer-Supported Collaborative Learning* 2(1):105–218.

Rourke, L., and Kanuka, H. (2009) "Learning in communities of inquiry: A review of the literature." *Journal of Distance Education* 23(1):19–48.

Rovai, A. (2002) "Building a sense of community at a distance." *International Review of Research in Open and Distance Learning* 3(1). Available at: http://www.irrodl.org/index.php/irrodl/article/view/79/153

Rovai, A. (2003) "A practical framework for evaluating online distance education programs." *Internet and Higher Education* 6(2):109–24.

Rüschoff, B., and Ritter, M. (2001) "Technology-enhanced language learning: Construction of knowledge and template-based learning in the foreign language classroom." *Computer Assisted Language Learning* 14(3/4):219–232.

Säljö, R. (1979) *Learning in the learner's perspective 1: Some commonplace misconceptions.* Reports from the Institute of Education 76. Gothenburg: University of Gothenburg.

Salmon, G. (2002) *E-tivities: The key to active online learning.* London: Kogan Page.

Salmon, G. (2004) *E-moderating: The key to teaching and learning online.* 2nd edn. London: Kogan Page.

Seale, J. (2003) *Learning technology in transition.* Lisse: Swets & Zeitlinger.

Sharples, M. (2007) "An interactional model of context". Presentation at the Philosophy of Technology-Enhanced Learning seminar, London Knowledge Lab, 29 June 2007.

Shih, M., Feng, J., and Tsai, C-C. (2008) "Research and trends in the field of e-learning from 2001 to 2005: A content analysis of cognitive studies in selected journals." *Computers & Education* 51(2):955–67.

Shulman, L. (1986) "Those who understand: Knowledge growth in teaching." *Educational Researcher* 15(2):4–14.

Shulman, L., and Shulman, J. (2004) "How and what teachers learn: A shifting perspective" *Journal of Curriculum Studies* 36(2):257–71.

Slevin, J. (2008) "E-learning and the transformation of social interaction in higher education." *Learning, Media and Technology* 33(2):115–26.

Smith, B. (2003) "Computer-mediated negotiated interaction: An expanded model." *The Modern Language Journal* 87(1):38–54.

Snyder, I. (1998) *Page to screen.* London: Routledge.

Snyder, I. (2002) *Silicon literacies: Communication, innovation and education in the Electronic Age.* London: Routledge.

Stahl, G. (2006) *Group cognition: Computer support for building collaborative knowledge.* Cambridge, MA: MIT Press.

Star, S., and Ruhleder, K. (1996) "Steps towards an ecology of infrastructure: Design and access for large information spaces." *Information Systems Research* 7(1):111–34.

Steffens, K. (2006) "Self-regulated learning in technology-enhanced learning environments: Lessons of a European peer review." *European Journal of Education* 41(3–4):353–79.

Strijbos, J.-W., Martens, R., Prins, F., and Jochems, W. (2006) "Content analysis: What are they talking about?" *Computers & Education* 46(1):29–48.

Suler, J. (2004) "The online disinhibition effect." *Cyber-psychology and Behaviour* 7(3):321–6.

Suler, J., and Phillips, W. (1998) "The bad boys of cyberspace: Deviant behaviour in multimedia chat communities." *Cyber-psychology and Behaviour* 1(2):275–94.

Suthers, D. (2006) "Technology affordances for intersubjective learning: A thematic agenda for CSCL." In Koschmann, T., Suthers, D., and Chan, T. (eds) *Computer supported collaborative learning: The next 10 years!* Mahwah, NJ: Lawrence Erlbaum, pp. 662–71.

Turoff, M., Hiltz, S., Bieber, M., Fjermestad, J., and Rana, A. (1999) "Collaborative discourse structures in computer mediated group communications." *Journal of Computer Mediated Communication* 4(4). Available at http://jcmc.indiana.edu/vol4/issue4/turoff.html.

Valcke, M., and Martens, R. (2006) "The problem arena of researching computer supported collaborative learning." *Computers & Education* 46(1):1–5.

Vaughan, N., and Garrison, R. (2007) "How blended learning can support faculty development community of inquiry." *Journal of Asynchronous Learning Networks* 10(4):139–52.

Vavoula, G., Pachler, N., and Kukulska-Hulme, A. (2009) (eds) *Researching mobile learning: Frameworks, tools and research designs.* Oxford: Peter Lang.

Veerman, A., Andriessen, J., and Kanselaar, G. (2000) "Learning through synchronous electronic discussion." *Computers & Education* 34(3–4):269–90.

Vygotsky, L. (1986) *Thought and language.* Cambridge, MA: MIT Press.

Warschauer, M. (1997) "Computer-mediated collaborative learning: Theory and practice." *The Modern Language Journal* 81(4):470–81.

Warschauer, M. (1999) *Electronic literacies: Language, culture and power in online education.* Lawrence Erlbaum Associates.

Wenger, E. (1998) *Communities of Practice: Learning, meaning, and identity.* Cambridge: Cambridge University Press.

Whitelock, D., and Jelfs, A. (2003) "Editorial." *Journal of Educational Media* 28(2–3):99–100.

Wiggins, G. (2001) *Educative assessment.* San Francisco, CA: Jossey-Bass.

Xin, C., and Feenberg, A. (2007) "Pedagogy in cyberspace: The dynamics of online discourse." *E–Learning* 4(4):415–32.

Zhao, Y., and Frank, K. (2003) "Factors affecting technology uses in schools: An ecological perspective." *American Educational Research Journal* 40(4):807–40.

Index

affinity groups 87
affordance 83, 100
amplification 8
approach, template-based 92–3
artefacts, digital 25, 87
assessment 86
  contribution of technology
  to 115–16

being an e-learner 29–32, 111
boundaries
  dissolving 42, 51, 89, 147

challenges
  for e-learners 132, 144, 146–7
  for schools, post-16 colleges and
  universities 54–5, 108
change
  cultural, economic,
  technological 3, 32, 37–55, 130
co-evolutionary model 134–5
cognition 87, 61–2, 79, 140
  distributed 87–8
cognitive change 136–8
collaboration 85
  scripts 99
common ground 89–90
community 67–71
  of inquiry (COI) 6, 68, 94–5,
  103–4, 106, 141–3
  of practice (COP) 39, 68, 87–8
computer-mediated communication
  (CMC) 32–3, 41, 64–7

computer-supported collaborative
  learning (CSCL) 34–5, 88–9, 99
computing
  ubiquitous 14, 42
conceptual development 33–4,
  66–7, 71
context-making 52–3, 74–5
contingency, moment of 116
Conversational Framework 25–6,
  63–4
CPD 92
cultures of use 99
cyberlearning 3

Digital Britain 5, 45
discourse analysis 86, 137
discourses 13
  unhelpful 1–2

disruption 2, 13, 62
distance education 6

e-assessment 111–27
  formative 114–19
ecology 38–40, 133
"Ecology of Resources" 63
e-facilitation 95
e-learning
  1.0 32
  2.0 32–3, 41–3, 73–4
  activity 20
  adoption 21, 51

asynchronous 32, 84, 64–7, 84
   benefits of 19, 23–4
   definitions of 15–16, 25
   design of 75–7, 87
   design principles 97–100
   drivers for 22
   evaluation of 110–11, 146–7
   strategy 14, 19–20, 46–7
   synchronous 32, 84
   theories of 18–19, 57–79
e-moderation 95
epistemic conflict 62, 64, 85
e-portfolio 72–3, 121–5
   definition of 123
   function of 123–4
ethics 60, 73, 144
ethnomethodology 86
European Commission 46

feedback, principles of 112–15

Horizon Report 4, 44, 47–8

identity 72–4, 82, 111, 144
   academic 84
   congruence 30–31
infrastructure
   relational 89
intentionality 7
interaction 42–3, 52–3, 61–3, 67,
   69, 74, 83

knowledge
   building 35, 85, 107
   construction 61–3, 87, 138

learner experiences 44, 139, 145
learning
   about 86
   as conversation 26
   blended 12–13
   community 14, 32
   definition of 11
   distance 12
   in formal and informal
   settings 82

internet-based 12
intersubjective 88–9
mixed-mode 14
mobile 14, 43
networked 14
online 11, 81–108
portfolio-based 124–5
pre-fixes of 16
professional 9, 92, 94, 97
psychological principles of
   101–2
spaces 91
theory 57–79, 81
technology-enhanced (TEL) 4,
   14
to be 86, 108
learning technologists 5
London Pedagogy Planner 92–3

MacArthur Report 44, 53
Master of Teaching (MTeach) 14,
   84, 94
meaning-making 17, 25, 26, 85,
   86, 88, 89
mobile complex 3

narrative 41–2, 72–3, 85, 98, 110
narrative turn 138–40

online
   communities 70–71, 85
   participation 67–71, 85–6, 88

pedagogy 16, 49–50
Phoebe 92
place
   making 91
   sense of 90–1
plagiarism 126
policy-making 43, 44, 45–9
policy tensions 49–50
portable devices 5
potential 3
practitioner development 38–9, 49,
   75–8

Qualitative Content Analysis
   (QCA)   140–43
quality assurance and
   enhancement   109–10

reduction   8
representation   117
   self-   72
resources
   conceptual   17
   semiotic   17

scaffolding   69, 113
selectivity   7
self-disclosure   72, 84
self-regulation   28–9, 111–14
sense-making   42, 98
social media   5
socio-cultural ecology   26–8
socio-cultural practices   43–5
sociogenic   40, 60
subjectivity   82

teaching text   83
technological pedagogical content
knowledge (TPCK)   76–8

technologies
   display   42–3
   mediating   4
   mobile   14, 28, 42–3
   sensor   42
   wireless   5
technology
   potential of   21–2
templates
   pedagogical   91–107
theory–practice relationship   145–7
tools   33–4
training
   computer-based (CBT)   11
   online   5
   web-based (WBT)   11
transformation   25, 60, 61–6, 72,
   75, 83, 135

Web 2.0   41–2, 73–4

Zone of Proximal Development
(ZPD)   34, 63